TEACHER'S PET PUBLICATIONS

LITPLAN TEACHER PACK
for
Mrs. Frisby and the Rats of NIMH
based on the book by
Robert C. O'Brien

Written by
Maggie Magno & Peter Sullivan

© 2008 Teacher's Pet Publications
All Rights Reserved

ISBN 978-1-60249-084-0

Copyright Teacher's Pet Publications 2008

Only the student materials in this unit plan (such as worksheets,
study questions, and tests) may be reproduced multiple times
for use in the purchaser's classroom.

For any additional copyright questions,
contact Teacher's Pet Publications.

www.tpet.com

TABLE OF CONTENTS
Mrs. Frisby and the Rats of NIMH

Introduction	5
Unit Objectives	7
Reading Assignment Sheet	8
Unit Outline	9
Study Questions (Short Answer)	13
Quiz/Study Questions (Multiple Choice	27
Pre-reading Vocabulary Worksheets	53
Lesson One (Introductory Lesson)	79
Non-fiction Assignment Sheet	81
Oral Reading Evaluation Form	84
Writing Assignment 1	91
Writing Assignment 2	96
Writing Assignment 3	100
Writing Evaluation Form	92
Vocabulary Review Activities	101
Extra Writing Assignments/Discussion ?s	103
Unit Review Activities	107
Unit Tests	113
Unit Resource Materials	177
Vocabulary Resource Materials	197

ABOUT THE AUTHOR

Robert C. O'Brien

Robert C. O'Brien was the pen name for Robert Leslie Conly, an American author and journalist for National Geographic. Born January 11, 1918, he was the third of five children. Shortly after his birth, his well-educated Irish-Catholic family moved from Brooklyn, New York to Amityville, Long Island where he later attended parochial school. As a child, he suffered from illness and nervousness. Conly sought comfort from his childhood difficulties in his love of music. He was adept at singing and piano playing.

He had an interest in both music and literature. Conly studied for a time at Juilliard, but ultimately went on to receive his Bachelor of Arts in English at the University of Rochester. Eventually, he became a journalist and writer.

He married Sarah McCaslin in 1943. This marriage lasted until his death thirty years later. Their daughter, Jane Leslie Conly, later published two novels based upon her father's characters.

Conly died at the age of 55 on March 5, 1973 in Washington, D.C. His wife and daughter finished his final book based on Conly's notes and published under his pseudonym, Robert C. O'Brien.

In 1982, *Mrs. Frisby and the Rats of NIMH* was made into an animated film, *The Secret of NIMH*.

Major Works
The Silver Crown (1968) *Mrs. Frisby and the Rats of NIMH* (1971) *A Report from Group 17* (1972) *Z for Zachariah* (1975)

Awards
1972 Newbery Medal (*Mrs. Frisby and the Rats of NIMH*)

1976 Edgar Award from the Mystery Writers of American for Best Juvenile Mystery

INTRODUCTION *Mrs. Frisby And The Rats Of NIMH*

This LitPlan has been designed to develop students' reading, writing, thinking, and language skills through exercises and activities related to *Mrs. Frisby and the Rats of NIMH*. It includes nineteen lessons, supported by extra resource materials.

The **introductory lesson** introduces students to animal rights and the pros and cons of using animals for testing. Following the introductory activity, students are given a transition to explain how the activity relates to the book they are about to read. Following the transition, students are given the materials they will be using during the unit. At the end of the lesson, students begin the pre-reading work for the first reading assignment.

The **reading assignments** are approximately twenty pages each; some are a little shorter while others are a little longer. Students have approximately 15 minutes of pre-reading work to do prior to each reading assignment. This pre-reading work involves reviewing the study questions for the assignment and doing some vocabulary work for 8 to 10 vocabulary words they will encounter in their reading.

The **study guide questions** are fact-based questions; students can find the answers to these questions right in the text. These questions come in two formats: short answer or multiple choice. The best use of these materials is probably to use the short answer version of the questions as study guides for students (since answers will be more complete), and to use the multiple choice version for occasional quizzes.

The **vocabulary work** is intended to enrich students' vocabularies as well as to aid in the students' understanding of the book. Prior to each reading assignment, students will complete a two-part worksheet for approximately 8 to 10 vocabulary words in the upcoming reading assignment. Part I focuses on students' use of general knowledge and contextual clues by giving the sentence in which the word appears in the text. Students are then to write down what they think the words mean based on the words' usage. Part II nails down the definitions of the words by giving students dictionary definitions of the words and having students match the words to the correct definitions based on the words' contextual usage. Students should then have an understanding of the words when they meet them in the text.

After each reading assignment, students will go back and formulate answers for the study guide questions. Discussion of these questions serves as a **review** of the most important events and ideas presented in the reading assignments.

After students complete reading the work, there is a **vocabulary review** lesson which pulls together all of the fragmented vocabulary lists for the reading assignments and gives students a review of all of the words they have studied.

Following the vocabulary review, a lesson is devoted to the **extra discussion questions/writing assignments**. These questions focus on interpretation, critical analysis, and personal response, employing a variety of thinking skills and adding to the students' understanding of the novel.

There is an **group theme project** in this unit. Students will break up into groups and create their ideal community just like the rats do in *Mrs. Frisby and the Rats of NIMH*.

There are three **writing assignments** in this unit, each with the purpose of informing, persuading, or expressing personal opinions. In Writing Assignment #1, students compare and contrast a character from the story and its real life animal equivalent. In Writing Assignment #2, students write Nicodemus's memoirs about the adventures he encountered after leaving the Boniface

Estate but before settling on the farm. Finally, in Writing Assignment #3, students persuade the rat community to either support Jenner's argument or Nicodemus's.

There is a **non-fiction reading assignment**. Students must read non-fiction articles, books, etc. to gather information about their themes in our world today.

The **review lesson** pulls together all of the aspects of the unit. The teacher is given four or five choices of activities or games to use which all serve the same basic function of reviewing all of the information presented in the unit.

The **unit test** comes in two formats: multiple choice or short answer. As a convenience, two different tests for each format have been included. There is also an advanced short answer unit test for advanced students.

There are additional **support materials** included with this unit. The **Unit Resource Materials** section includes suggestions for an in-class library, crossword and word search puzzles related to the novel, and extra worksheets. There is a list of **bulletin board ideas** which gives the teacher suggestions for bulletin boards to go along with this unit. In addition, there is a list of **extra class activities** the teacher could choose from to enhance the unit or as a substitution for an exercise the teacher might feel is inappropriate for his/her class. **Answer keys** are located directly after the **reproducible student materials** throughout the unit. The **Vocabulary Resource Materials** section includes similar worksheets and games to reinforce the vocabulary words.

The **level** of this unit can be varied depending upon the criteria on which the individual assignments are graded, the teacher's expectations of his/her students in class discussions, and the formats chosen for the study guides, quizzes and test. If teachers have other ideas/activities they wish to use, they can usually easily be inserted prior to the review lesson.

The student materials may be reproduced for use in the teacher's classroom without infringement of copyrights. No other portion of this unit may be reproduced without the written consent of Teacher's Pet Publications, Inc.

UNIT OBJECTIVES *Mrs. Frisby And The Rats Of NIMH*

1. Students will practice reading orally and silently.

2. Students will answer questions to demonstrate their knowledge and understanding of the main events and characters in *Mrs. Frisby and the Rats of NIMH*.

3. Students will study vocabulary from the book to better understand the book and to enrich their own vocabularies.

4. Students will read aloud, report, and participate in large and small group discussions to improve their public speaking and personal interaction skills.

5. Students will create their own ideal communities and present their creation to the class through an oral presentation.

6. Students will work together in a cooperative group.

7. Students will read non-fiction text that relates to *Mrs. Frisby and the Rats of NIMH* and will present it to the class.

8. The writing assignments in this unit are designed for several purposes:

    a. To check and increase students reading comprehension.

    b. To make students think about the ideas presented by the novel

    c. To encourage logical thinking

    d. To provide an opportunity to practice good grammar and improve students' use of the English language.

    e. To encourage students' creativity

READING ASSIGNMENTS *Mrs. Frisby And The Rats Of NIMH*

Date Assigned	Assignment	Completion Date
	Assignment 1 The Sickness of Timothy Frisby & Mr. Ages	
	Assignment 2 The Crow and the Cat, Mr. Fitzgibbon's Plow, & Five Days	
	Assignment 3 A Favor from Jeremy, The Owl, & "Go to the Rats"	
	Assignment 4 In the Rosebush, Brutus, & In the Library	
	Assignment 5 Isabella, A Powder for Dragon, & The Marketplace	
	Assignment 6 In the Cage & The Maze	
	Assignment 7 A Lesson in Reading & The Air Ducts	
	Assignment 8 The Boniface Estate, The Main Hall, & The Toy Tinker	
	Assignment 9 Thorn Valley & Captured	
	Assignment 10 Seven Dead Rats & Escape	
	Assignment 11 At the Meeting, The Doctor, & Epilogue	

UNIT OUTLINE *Mrs. Frisby And The Rats Of NIMH*

1 Introduction Group Theme Project	2 PVR 1	3 Study ?s 1 PVR 2 Conflict Types	4 Study ?s 2 PVR 3 Non-fiction Reading Assignment	5 Study ?s 3 PVR 4 Character Analysis
6 Study ?s 4 PVR 5	7 Study ?s 5 PVR 6 Writing Assignment #1	8 Study ?s 6 PVR 7	9 Study ?s 7 PVR 8 Writing Conferences	10 Study ?s 8 PVR 9 Writing Assignment #2
11 Study ?s 9 PVR 10	12 Study ?s 10 PVR 11 Writing Conferences	13 Study ?s 11 Writing Assignment #3	14 Vocabulary Review	15 Extra Discussion Questions
16 Discussion of Non fiction Assignment	17 Presentation of Community Projects	18 Unit Review	19 Unit Test	

Key: P = Preview Study Questions   V = Vocabulary Work   R = Read

STUDY GUIDE QUESTIONS

STUDY GUIDE QUESTIONS *Mrs. Frisby And The Rats Of NIMH*

Assignment 1
The Sickness of Timothy Frisby & Mr. Ages

1. Describe Mrs. Frisby's house.
2. Why are January and February the hardest months for Mrs. Frisby and her children?
3. Why is Mrs. Frisby depressed when she looks in her pantry for food?
4. What does Mrs. Frisby find in the hole in the tree stump?
5. What are the symptoms of Timothy's illness?
6. Why does Mrs. Frisby worry about the trip to see Mr. Ages and why does she eventually go?
7. From what does Mr. Ages make his draughts and powders?
8. What was the purpose of Mrs. Frisby's first visit to Mr. Ages?
9. Describe the interior of Mr. Ages's house.
10. What illness does Mr. Ages diagnose Timothy with, and what does he give to Mrs. Frisby?

Assignment 2
The Crow and the Cat, Mr. Fitzgibbon's Plow, & Five Days

1. Identify and describe Dragon.
2. Identify Jeremy.
3. What did Mr. Frisby used to say about the size of an animal's brain?
4. What upcoming event forces Mrs. Frisby to take risks and seek help?
5. Why must all the animals move out of the garden when winter is over?
6. Why didn't the Frisbys make their winter home in the barn lofts or attics like some other field mice?
7. Why is the thawing frost a problem for the Frisbys?
8. How long does Farmer Fitzgibbon say he will wait to plow? Why?
9. After Mrs. Frisby runs from Dragon and climbs the dead asparagus plant, what does she see beyond the cat?

Assignment 3
A Favor from Jeremy, The Owl, & "Go to the Rats"

1. Who is the oldest animal in the woods, and where does he live?
2. What convinces Mrs. Frisby to go see the owl?
3. According to Jeremy what is the best time to see the owl? Why?
4. Why is Timothy not told his mother is going to see the owl?
5. Why does Mrs. Frisby hesitate before entering the owl's house?
6. What is the owl's advice to Mrs. Frisby?
7. According to Jeremy, what does "in the lee" mean?

Assignment 4
<u>In the Rosebush, Brutus, & In the Library</u>
1. How does Timothy know that Moving Day is near?
2. Why doesn't Dragon follow animals into the rose bush?
3. How does Mrs. Frisby enter the rosebush?
4. Mrs. Frisby encounters someone she knows in the rose bush. Who? Why is he limping?
5. Describe Justin.
6. Describe what astonishes Mrs. Frisby when she turns the corner of the dark corridor in the rat hole.
7. Where do the rats get their lights, and why do they get the small ones?
8. What does Mrs. Frisby notice about Nicodemus when she meets him?
9. Where does Justin take Mrs. Frisby to wait for the meeting to end, and what does she find on the blackboard?

Assignment 5
<u>Isabella, A Powder for Dragon, & The Marketplace</u>
1. Why does Mrs. Frisby decide against leaving the library to look around?
2. Who or what does Isabella think Mrs. Frisby is?
3. What does Mrs. Frisby learn from Isabella about life in the rat colony?
4. Who is Arthur?
5. What does Nicodemus take from his satchel to help him see, and why does he need it?
6. According to Nicodemus, what did the owl mean by moving her house "in the lee" of the stone?
7. According to Justin, what do the rats do about Dragon when they have a long project?
8. How do the rats get the powder into Dragon's dish?
9. Describe the object in Nicodemus's office that particularly attracts Mrs. Frisby's attention.
10. With whom did Nicodemus usually go to the market? Why?

Assignment 6
<u>In the Cage & The Maze</u>
1. After the men catch the rats, what do they say about the rats and their ability to communicate?
2. Where do the men take Nicodemus, Jenner, and the other rats?
3. Describe Nicodemus's cage. Why does he dislike it so much?
4. According to Nicodemus, what do the rats eventually learn after their initial fear and uncertainty?
5. How does Dr. Schultz organize the rats?
6. According to Nicodemus, what is the reason for their captivity?
7. Describe Nicodemus's first experience in the Maze.
8. What happens after Nicodemus runs the Maze more often? Why does he still run through it?
9. Describe the "shape recognition" test.

10. What does Julie do when Justin runs away the first time?

Assignment 7
<u>A Lesson in Reading & The Air Ducts</u>
1. What were the injections doing to Group A?
2. What were Dr. Schultz and his assistants attempting to do when they showed the rats a picture of a rat and symbols while playing a recording that said "Are, Aie, Tea, Rat"?
3. How did Justin get out of his cage after the doctor and his assistants went home for the night?
4. Why didn't Justin want Nicodemus to explore the laboratory with him?
5. Why did the rats steal a spool of thread to help them explore the ducts?
6. What does Jonathan the mouse ask Nicodemus?
7. What does Nicodemus decide regarding whether or not the mice can come with the rats?
8. What are Jenner's concerns regarding what the rats would do after they escaped?
9. What happens to six of the eight mice in the air duct?
10. How did the mice help save the rats?

Assignment 8
<u>The Boniface Estate, The Main Hall, & The Toy Tinker</u>
1. How did the rats know the Boniface Estate was deserted before entering the house?
2. How did the rats keep themselves from being detected by the caretaker-gardener?
3. What did the rats do late into the night all winter long while staying at the Boniface Estate?
4. What does Justin show Mrs. Frisby when she returns to the rosebush in the late afternoon?
5. What is "The Plan"?
6. Explain the differences between the evolution of rats and monkeys according to one of the books that Nicodemus read.
7. The rats read many books while staying at the Boniface house. What kind of books were difficult to find?
8. Why are rats the most hated animals on earth, according to Nicodemus?
9. After they left the Boniface Estate, where did the rats want their new home to be? Why?
10. How did the Toy Tinker die?

Assignment 9
<u>Thorn Valley & Captured</u>
1. Describe what Nicodemus and the rats found in the Toy Tinker's truck.
2. How did the rats get running water and electricity?
3. What is a "rat race"?
4. What is the result of Mrs. Jones's purchasing a vacuum?
5. How did Nicodemus become acquainted with the owl?

6. Why do Nicodemus and most of the other rats want to leave their current location and start over?
7. Why didn't Jonathan Frisby tell his wife about NIMH?
8. What happened to Jenner?
9. Why do the rats want to destroy the machinery and the other conveniences of their current home?
10. What happens to Mrs. Frisby after she puts the sleeping draught into Dragon's bowl?

Assignment 10
Seven Dead Rats & Escape
1. Who is Porgy?
2. What was Paul trying to convince Billy to do, and what is his argument?
3. What happened at Henderson's Hardware Store?
4. Why did the federal government send a squad with a truckload of equipment to the hardware store?
5. Why do Paul and Mr. Fitzgibbon believe the Public Health Service is so concerned about the rats?
6. Why doesn't Justin simply open the door of Mrs. Frisby's cage?
7. Why does Justin believe Mrs. Frisby has brought the rats good luck?
8. Who does Justin believe the seven dead rats are?
9. What is the problem the rats encounter while trying to move Mrs. Frisby's house?
10. What are some of the things the rats did in order to move Mrs. Frisby's house?

Assignment 11
At the Meeting, The Doctor, & Epilogue
1. Why does Brutus come to find Mrs. Frisby?
2. Who does Nicodemus believe is coming to get the rats?
3. What did the rats do to make the exterminators believe it was an ordinary rat hole?
4. Why is Mrs. Frisby concerned that only seven rats exited the cave at first?
5. What do the seven rats do to trick the exterminators?
6. Who was the 8th rat that left the rat hole and fell unconscious?
7. Who do the children believe went back into the hole to save the rat who had fallen?
8. Where do the Frisbys live in the summer?
9. Why does Mrs. Frisby decide to tell the children about NIMH?
10. What does Martin want to do in the fall? Why?

STUDY GUIDE QUESTIONS ANSWER KEY *Mrs. Frisby And The Rats Of NIMH*

The Sickness of Timothy Frisby & Mr. Ages

1. Describe Mrs. Frisby's house.
   It is a slightly damaged cinder block, the hollow kind with two oval holes through it. It is almost completely buried with only a bit of one corner showing above ground. It sits on its side in such a way that the solid parts of the block forms a roof and a floor, both waterproof, and the hollows make two spacious rooms. The interior is lined with bits of leaves, grass, cloth, cotton fluff, and other soft things keeping it dry during the winter. A tunnel to the surface lets in air and sunlight but is too small for a cat's paw to fit through. Another tunnel is underground and connects the two rooms.

2. Why are January and February the hardest months for Mrs. Frisby and her children?
   January and February are the hardest months; the sharp, hard cold begins in December and lasts until March. By February all the beans and black-eyed peas are picked over (with help from the birds), the asparagus roots are frozen into stone, and the potatoes are frozen and unfrozen so many times they acquire a slimy texture and rancid taste.

3. Why is Mrs. Frisby depressed when she looks in her pantry for food?
   The food is the same tiresome fare her family eats every day. She wishes she could find a bit of green lettuce, or a small egg, or a taste of cheese, or a corn muffin to add variety to their food supply.

4. What does Mrs. Frisby find in the hole in the tree stump?
   She finds not the green lettuce she had hoped for, but eight large ears of corn, some fresh peanuts, some hickory nuts, and a stack of dried, sweet smelling mushrooms.

5. What are the symptoms of Timothy's illness?
   At first his forehead is hot and damp with sweat and his pulse is alarmingly fast. He feels cold, gets dizzy when he sits up, and cannot breathe very well. By lunchtime his condition is much worse. His eyes are wild and strange from fever, he trembles continuously, moans and gasps for breath. He has nightmares, but when his family talks to him he cannot hear them and stares past them as if they are not present.

6. Why does Mrs. Frisby worry about the trip to see Mr. Ages and why does she eventually go?
   The trip is a long, hard journey that is risky unless she is extremely cautious. She cannot take the shortest route because it would lead her too close to the farmhouse and the barn, where the cat stalks relentlessly. Ordinarily, she does not set out so late in the day, for fear that darkness will come too soon. She decides to leave because Timothy is so sick she obviously cannot wait until the next day.

7. From what does Mr. Ages make his draughts and powders?
   He makes them from the stalks and seeds and pods of weeds and other plants around his home.

8. What was the purpose of Mrs. Frisby's first visit to Mr. Ages?
   Timothy wandered away while playing with the other children and was bitten by a poisonous spider. Mrs. Frisby and her husband carried him to Mr. Ages, who gave him a milky liquid to "unlock" his muscles and treat his symptoms.

9. Describe the interior of Mr. Ages's house.
   It is somewhat larger than a shoe box (but about the same shape) and resembles the house of a hermit. It is bare of furniture except for a bit of bedding in one corner, a stool made of a piece of brick, and another piece of brick worn smooth from use as a pestle on which he grinds his medicines. Along one entire wall, arranged neatly in small piles, stand the raw materials he collects: roots, seeds, dried leaves, pods, strips of bark, and shriveled mushrooms.

10. What illness does Mr. Ages diagnose Timothy with, and what does he give to Mrs. Frisby?
    He diagnoses Timothy with pneumonia and gives her three packets of medicine, powders neatly wrapped in white paper. He tells her to keep Timothy warm and to make him stay in bed.

The Crow and the Cat, Mr. Fitzgibbon's Plow, & Five Days
1. Identify and describe Dragon.
    Dragon is Farmer Fitzgibbon's cat. He is enormous, with a huge, broad head and a large mouth full of curving fangs, needle sharp. He has seven claws on each foot and a thick, furry tail, which lashes angrily from side to side. In color he is orange and white, with glaring yellow eyes.
2. Identify Jeremy.
    Jeremy is a crow that befriends Mrs. Frisby after she saves him from Dragon.
3. What did Mr. Frisby used to say about the size of an animal's brain?
    The size of the brain is no measure of its capacity.
4. What upcoming event forces Mrs. Frisby to take risks and seek help?
    Mrs. Frisby needs help and advice because Moving Day is coming soon, and Timothy is not well enough to be moved.
5. Why must all the animals move out of the garden when winter is over?
    As soon as the weather allows, Farmer Fitzgibbon's tractor comes rumbling through, pulling the sharp-bladed plow through the soil, turning over every foot of it. No animal caught in the garden that day is likely to escape alive.
6. Why didn't the Frisbys make their winter home in the barn lofts or attics like some other field mice?
    The Frisbys always go to the garden, preferring the relative safety and freedom of the outdoors.
7. Why is the thawing frost a problem for the Frisbys?
    Farmer Fitzgibbon plows when the last frost is gone, and the Frisbys' home will be in jeopardy when the plow comes through.
8. How long does Farmer Fitzgibbon say he will wait to plow? Why?
    Farmer Fitzgibbon says he will wait five days to plow because he needs to order a new linch pin from Henderson's. Also it is too wet to plow, but five continuous days of sun should dry the ground out.
9. After Mrs. Frisby runs from Dragon and climbs the dead asparagus plant, what does she see beyond the cat?
    She sees a dozen rats moving a long piece of electric cable, the heavy, black kind used for outdoor wiring and strung on telephone poles.

A Favor from Jeremy, The Owl, & "Go to the Rats"
1. Who is the oldest animal in the woods, and where does he live?
    The owl is the oldest animal in the woods. He lives about a mile from Mrs. Frisby in a hollow at the top of a large Beech tree, the biggest tree in the whole forest.
2. What convinces Mrs. Frisby to go see the owl?
    She thinks of Timothy and the big plow blade. She tells herself she has no choice and if there is any chance that the owl might help her she must go.

3. According to Jeremy what is the best time to see the owl? Why?
   The best time to see him is just at dusk. When the light gets dim, he comes to the entrance of the hollow and watches while the dark comes in. That's the time to ask him questions.
4. Why is Timothy not told his mother is going to see the owl?
   Timothy is not told about the expedition lest he worry and blame himself for the risk his mother must take.
5. Why does Mrs. Frisby hesitate before entering the owl's house?
   She knows something of the dietary habits of owls, and she does not much like the idea of being trapped in his house.
6. What is the owl's advice to Mrs. Frisby?
   He tells her to go see the rats. She should tell Justin, the sentry guarding the door, who she is--and she should ask to see a rat named Nicodemus. The owl recommends doing whatever the rats ask of her.
7. According to Jeremy, what does "in the lee" mean?
   It means the calm side, the side the wind does not blow from. He says when there is a strong wind, you fly up to the barn from the lee, so you don't get bashed into the wall.

In the Rosebush, Brutus, & In the Library
1. How does Timothy know that Moving Day is near?
   Timothy knows that Moving Day is near because he can smell the frost melting. He remembers that they moved shortly after he smelled it the previous year.
2. Why doesn't Dragon follow animals into the rose bush?
   Dragon chases animals to the edge of the bush but does not follow them in. The thorns help to discourage trespassers.
3. How does Mrs. Frisby enter the rosebush?
   She notices that on one branch, close to the ground, the thorns are scraped off, and about a half inch of it--just big enough for a handhold--is worn smooth. She pushes the branch timidly and it opens like a swinging door.
4. Mrs. Frisby encounters someone she knows in the rose bush. Who? Why is he limping?
   She encounters Mr. Ages. He is limping because he had a bad fall and broke his ankle.
5. Describe Justin.
   He looks alert, dark gray in color, and is extraordinarily handsome, though not as huge as Brutus.
6. Describe what astonishes Mrs. Frisby when she turns the corner of the dark corridor in the rat hole.
   Ahead of her stretches a long, well-lit hallway. Its ceiling and walls are a smoothly curved arch, its floor hard and flat, with a soft layer of carpet down the middle. The light comes from the walls, where every foot or so on both sides a tiny light bulb is recessed in the hole in which it stands, like a small window, is covered with a square of colored glass-- blue, green, or yellow. The effect is that of stained-glass windows in sunlight.
7. Where do the rats get their lights, and why do they get the small ones?
   They find the lights on trees. In fact, most of their lights come from trees. They find them mostly after Christmas around New Year's. They get the small lights because they have difficulty handling the large ones.

8. What does Mrs. Frisby notice about Nicodemus when she meets him?
   She notices that he speaks graciously, with an air of dignity. He has a scar on his face that runs across his left eye that has a black patch over it, fastened by a cord around his head. He also carries a satchel--rather like a hand-bag--by a strap over his shoulders.
9. Where does Justin take Mrs. Frisby to wait for the meeting to end, and what does she find on the blackboard?
   Justin takes Mrs. Frisby to the library to wait until the meeting is finished. She reads on the blackboard at the back of the room "THE PLAN OF THE RATS OF NIMH."

Isabella, A Powder for Dragon, & The Marketplace
1. Why does Mrs. Frisby decide against leaving the library to look around?
   She starts out into the hall, and then changes her mind. Nicodemus has been friendly--they all have been friendly--but explicit. He told her to wait in the library. She is not there to pry but to get help.
2. Who or what does Isabella think Mrs. Frisby is?
   Isabella thinks that Mrs. Frisby is a spy from outside or from NIMH.
3. What does Mrs. Frisby learn from Isabella about life in the rat colony?
   She learns that they have a grain room (presumable for food storage); the females sometimes go to meetings and sometimes not; Nicodemus seems to be the leader; they have a Plan for the future that some rats do not like; and one, named Jenner, has deserted.
4. Who is Arthur?
   He is a stocky, square, and muscular rat with bright, hard eyes. He looks efficient and Nicodemus tells Mrs. Frisby that one might call him the "chief engineer."
5. What does Nicodemus take from his satchel to help him see, and why does he need it?
   Nicodemus takes a reading glass from his satchel to help him see. When he lost his left eye, he also damaged his right one. He can see little close-up without the glass and not much more with it.
6. According to Nicodemus, what did the owl mean by moving her house "in the lee" of the stone?
   When a farmer plows a field with a big rock in it, he plows around the rock--close on each side, but leaving a triangle of unplowed land on each end. Mrs. Frisby's house is beside the rock and will get plowed up--and probably crushed, as the owl said. If the rats can move the house a few feet--so that it lies buried behind the rock--in the lee--then Mrs. Frisby and her children can stay in it as long as they need to.
7. According to Justin, what do the rats do about Dragon when they have a long project?
   To make sure Dragon won't bother them, they put sleeping powder in his food. Mr. Ages makes it. It does not do the cat any harm but makes him stay extremely drowsy for approximately eight hours. They station a sentry to watch him so they are free to work.
8. How do the rats get the powder into Dragon's dish?
   There is a very shallow space between the floor and the bottom of the cabinet in the Fitzgibbons' kitchen. There is a hole behind the cabinet that they previously cut. Mr. Ages usually crawls through the hole and underneath the cabinet, dashes out to Dragon's bowl, deposits the powder in his food, and dashes back through the hole.
9. Describe the object in Nicodemus's office that particularly attracts Mrs. Frisby's attention.
   Mrs. Frisby is particularly attracted to a box in the corner of Nicodemus's office. It has dials and a light shining on the front; from it comes the soft sound of music. It is a radio.

10. With whom did Nicodemus usually go to the market? Why?
    He usually went to the market with his older brother, Gerald, and his friend, Jenner. They were his two closest friends. They liked the same games, the same jokes, the same topics of conversation--even the same kinds of food.

In the Cage & The Maze
1. After the men catch the rats, what do they say about the rats and their ability to communicate?
   One tells the others that the rats can communicate and will inform the others about their experience. He says the rats will case the place carefully before they come again, but they will not come for a few more days. He also says they are lucky to have caught so many. The rats had not been bothered in so long they had grown careless.
2. Where do the men take Nicodemus, Jenner, and the other rats?
   The men take all the rats to a laboratory called NIMH.
3. Describe Nicodemus's cage. Why does he dislike it so much?
   It has a floor made of some kind of plastic, medium-soft and warm to the touch. With wire walls and ceiling, it is airy enough. The mere fact that it is a cage makes it horrible. He can only move three hops forward and back again. Worst of all, he hates the feeling that they are all at the mercy of someone they do not know.
4. According to Nicodemus, what do the rats eventually learn after their initial fear and uncertainty?
   They learn that uncertainty is the worst thing they will undergo. They are treated very well, except for small, quick flashes of pain that are part of their training. They are always well fed, although the food is not delicious by any means.
5. How does Dr. Schultz organize the rats?
   He splits them up into groups A, B, and C. There are twenty in group A, twenty in group B, and 23 in group C. The cages and collars for the rats are numbered accordingly. The rats in the A group will receive injections of series A and training. The rats in B will receive injections of series B and training. Group C will be the control group and only receive a prick from a plain needle.
6. According to Nicodemus, what is the reason for their captivity?
   Dr. Schultz is a neurologist--that is, an expert on brains, nerves, intelligence, and how people learn things. By experimenting on the rats, he hopes to find out whether certain injections can help them learn more and faster.
7. Describe Nicodemus's first experience in the Maze.
   He can see a corridor that leads to a green lawn outdoors. He must maneuver his way through the maze to get to there. If he goes down the wrong path he will feel an electric shock through the floor. However, right as he reaches the end of the Maze George picks him up.
8. What happens after Nicodemus runs the Maze more often? Why does he still run through it?
   Each time Nicodemus runs through the Maze his completion time is shorter. Julie, George, or Dr. Schultz picks him up at the end of the maze and writes down his time. Nicodemus understands that he will never get away. He runs through the Maze because he lives in a cage and cannot bear not to run, even if he is running toward an illusion.

9. Describe the "shape recognition" test.
   The rats are put into a small room with three doors leading out--one round, one square, and one triangular. The doors are on hinges, with springs to hold them shut, but they are easy to open. Each door leads into another room with three more doors like the first one. The trick is this: If you go through the wrong door, the room you enter has an electric floor and you get a shock. You have to learn: In the first room, you use the round door; the second room, triangle, and so on.

10. What does Julie do when Justin runs away the first time?
    She does not seem alarmed. She calmly places the needle on a shelf, walks to the door of the laboratory and pushes a button on the wall. A red light comes on, and she picks up a notebook and pencil and follows Justin around the laboratory.

A Lesson in Reading & The Air Ducts

1. What were the injections doing to Group A?
   The rats were becoming smarter than rats had ever been before, and the aging process seemed to stop almost completely.

2. What were Dr. Schultz and his assistants attempting to do when they showed the rats a picture of a rat and symbols while playing a recording that said "Are, Aie, Tea, Rat"?
   They were teaching the rats to read.

3. How did Justin get out of his cage after the doctor and his assistants went home for the night?
   Justin read the instructions on the bottom of the cage informing him how to open the door.

4. Why didn't Justin want Nicodemus to explore the laboratory with him?
   Justin wanted to be cautious. He wasn't sure if it was safe to be out of the cage and he didn't want Nicodemus to get into trouble. Justin knew the doctor would grow suspicious if he caught two rats out of their cages. It would indicate that the rats are smarter than the doctor knows.

5. Why did the rats steal a spool of thread to help them explore the ducts?
   The rats did not have a light to help them explore the maze of air ducts. They tied one end of the thread to the laboratory's air duct and unwound the thread as they explored. They used the thread to find their way back to the laboratory and to mark the passage they needed to take in order to escape.

6. What does Jonathan the mouse ask Nicodemus?
   Jonathan asks Nicodemus to open the cages of the mice and to allow them to escape with the rats.

7. What does Nicodemus decide regarding whether or not the mice can come with the rats?
   Nicodemus agrees to open the cages of the mice and allow them to follow them down the air duct, but tells them the mice are on their own once they escape.

8. What are Jenner's concerns regarding what the rats would do after they escaped?
   Jenner was concerned with where the rats would go once they escaped. He didn't think it was wise to go home again because they wouldn't fit in with the other rats. They had become something different and didn't want to live in sewer pipes or eat other people's garbage.

9. What happens to six of the eight mice in the air duct?
   Six of the eight mice were blown away by the great bursts of air. Jonathan and a white mouse were saved by Nicodemus and another rat.

10. How did the mice help save the rats?
    The white mouse had the rats pry a hole into the wire screen. Then he and Jonathan climbed through to the other side and figured out how to unlock the screen.

The Boniface Estate, The Main Hall, & The Toy Tinker
1. How did the rats know the Boniface Estate was deserted before entering the house?
   There were weeds in front of the entrance gate: no one had driven through it in a while. There was a padlock on the fence. There were automatic lights in the house that all came on at the same time to keep away burglars.
2. How did the rats keep themselves from being detected by the caretaker-gardener?
   They had to haul all their empty tin cans and other trash far from the house. They cleaned up after themselves carefully. They learned to use the water taps and the dusting cloths they found in the kitchen closet.
3. What did the rats do late into the night all winter long while staying at the Boniface Estate?
   They studied the books in the library and taught themselves to write.
4. What does Justin show Mrs. Frisby when she returns to the rosebush in the late afternoon?
   The natural cave that the rats have turned into a workshop dedicated to putting "The Plan" into action.
5. What is "The Plan"?
   The Plan is to live without stealing.
6. Explain the differences between the evolution of rats and monkeys according to one of the books that Nicodemus read.
   Millions of years ago rats seemed to be ahead of all the other animals. They were well-organized and built very complicated villages in the fields. But somehow it didn't work out. The scientist who wrote the book thought that it was because the rats' lives were too easy; while the other animals (like monkeys) were living in the woods and getting tougher and smarter, the rats grew soft and lazy and made no more progress. Eventually the monkeys came out of the woods, walking on their hind legs, and took over the prairies and almost everything else. It was then that the rats were driven to become scavengers and thieves, living on the fringes of a world run by men.
7. The rats read many books while staying at the Boniface house. What kind of books were difficult to find?
   Books about rats were difficult to find.
8. Why are rats the most hated animals on earth, according to Nicodemus?
   They are the most hated animals because they steal food.
9. After they left the Boniface Estate, where did the rats want their new home to be? Why?
   The rats wanted their new home to be near the mountains because there would be natural caves for them to live in. They also wanted to be near a farm so that they would have plenty of food nearby.
10. How did the Toy Tinker die?
    He had spent the night in the forest. His truck had become stuck in the mud. He tried to get it out of the mud, but the strain was too much for him. He died of a heart attack while he was on his way out of the forest to find help.

Thorn Valley & Captured

1. Describe what Nicodemus and the rats found in the Toy Tinker's truck.
   The rats found the Toy Tinker's tools. The tools were small enough for the rats to use.
2. How did the rats get running water and electricity?
   They obtained running water and electricity by stealing from Farmer Fitzgibbon. They tapped into his underground cable and water pipe.
3. What is a "rat race"?
   A "rat race" is a race where, no matter how fast you run, you don't get anywhere.
4. What is the result of Mrs. Jones's purchasing a vacuum?
   Because Mrs. Jones buys a vacuum, all the other housewives are jealous and want a vacuum too. In order to keep up with the vacuum demand, the manufacturer opens a factory. Due to the demand of electricity, the electric company opens a new plant and pollutes the air causing more dirt for the housewives to clean with their vacuums.
5. How did Nicodemus become acquainted with the owl?
   Nicodemus asked a chipmunk if he knew what was on the other side of the mountains. The chipmunk directed Nicodemus to the owl. The owl talked with Nicodemus because he was interested in the civilization built by the rats.
6. Why do Nicodemus and most of the other rats want to leave their current location and start over?
   They want to leave because they are afraid of getting caught, life had become too easy, and they feel bad about stealing from Mr. Fitzgibbon.
7. Why didn't Jonathan Frisby tell his wife about NIMH?
   Mr. Ages explains that Jonathan didn't want to hurt Mrs. Frisby. He knew he would stay young while she grew older and eventually would die. He was afraid the news would hurt her.
8. What happened to Jenner?
   Jenner left with some other rats who were against the Plan. He was especially angry about the decision to destroy all the machines. Jenner and his friends wanted to build another civilization like the one they left.
9. Why do the rats want to destroy the machinery and the other conveniences of their current home?
   The rats want to destroy the machinery because if the cave is later discovered, it would only look like debris, and their secret wouldn't be discovered. Also, they know their first few years in Thorn Valley are going to be difficult, and they want to remove the temptation to come back to their comfortable home.
10. What happens to Mrs. Frisby after she puts the sleeping draught into Dragon's bowl?
    Billy, the youngest Fitzgibbon, traps Mrs. Frisby under a colander.

Seven Dead Rats & Escape

1. Who is Porgy?
   Porgy was the Fitzgibbons' yellow canary who had died a few months earlier and who had been the occupant of the cage in which Mrs. Frisby was trapped.
2. What was Paul trying to convince Billy to do, and what is his argument?
   Paul wanted Billy to let Mrs. Frisby go. He believed she was frightened and would die because wild animals shouldn't be put into cages unless done so at an early age.
3. What happened at Henderson's Hardware Store?
   Six or seven rats got themselves electrocuted there while trying to move a motor.

4. Why did the federal government send a squad with a truckload of equipment to the hardware store?
   Fred Smith had written an article about the seven dead rats entitled "Mechanized Rats Invade Hardware Store."

5. Why do Paul and Mr. Fitzgibbon believe the Public Health Service is so concerned about the rats?
   They think the Public Health Service is concerned the rats are carrying rabies, and they are keeping it secret so people don't panic.

6. Why doesn't Justin simply open the door of Mrs. Frisby's cage?
   He decides not to simply open the door because Mrs. Frisby can't do such a thing on her own and the Fitzgibbons might grow suspicious. Instead, Justin makes it look like the cage is defective.

7. Why does Justin believe Mrs. Frisby has brought the rats good luck?
   Mrs. Frisby has heard about the exterminators that will be arriving the day after next and tells Justin about it in time for the rats to save themselves.

8. Who does Justin believe the seven dead rats are?
   Justin believes the rats are Jenner and his friends.

9. What is the problem the rats encounter while trying to move Mrs. Frisby's house?
   The shrew is standing between the house and the rats, refusing to let the rats move the house. She doesn't believe they have the permission of Mrs. Frisby because Mrs. Frisby is nowhere to be found. The shrew even bit Arthur on the leg to prevent him from commencing his work.

10. What are some of the things the rats did in order to move Mrs. Frisby's house?
    They used a scaffolding system and pulleys to lift the house. Then, they put round pieces of wood resembling sawed-off broom handles under the cinder block and rolled it like a truck to its new location. They also dug a hole precisely the size of the cinder block so that it would fit nicely in its new spot near the boulder. They used shovels to dig a new entrance to the house.

At the Meeting, The Doctor, & Epilogue

1. Why does Brutus come to find Mrs. Frisby?
   Nicodemus wants to see her because he wants to hear more about what Mr. Fitzgibbon said regarding the exterminators.

2. Who does Nicodemus believe is coming to get the rats?
   Men from NIMH.

3. What did the rats do to make the exterminators believe it was an ordinary rat hole?
   They moved all of their equipment to the cave and sealed it off. They ripped up all the carpet and wiring. They brought garbage into the storeroom. They destroyed the elegant archway. They dug a false back door.

4. Why is Mrs. Frisby concerned that only seven rats exited the cave at first?
   She knew ten rats had stayed behind as a rear guard and thought the other three may have been killed by the gas.

5. What do the seven rats do to trick the exterminators?
   They all run out at once. Then, they run out two or three at a time to make it look like dozens of rats are leaving the hole. In reality, most of the rats had left early in the morning.

6. Who was the 8th rat that left the rat hole and fell unconscious?
   Brutus

7. Who do the children believe went back into the hole to save the rat who had fallen?
   The children believe Justin was the rescuing rat because he was so brave and had gone back to save their mother.

8. Where do the Frisbys live in the summer?
   They live near a brook.

9. Why does Mrs. Frisby decide to tell the children about NIMH?
   She believes her children have a right to know about their father and the possibility that they might be different from other mice because of their father's injections.

10. What does Martin want to do in the fall? Why?
    He wants to ask Jeremy to take him to the rats in Thorn Valley because he wants to know if it was Justin who died in the rat hole.

MULTIPLE CHOICE STUDY/QUIZ QUESTIONS
Mrs. Frisby And The Rats Of NIMH

Assignment 1
The Sickness of Timothy Frisby & Mr. Ages

1. Which phrase does NOT describe Mrs. Frisby's house?
    A. Has two rooms
    B. Is lined with bits of leaves and soft things
    C. Is situated under the farm house
    D. Is in a cinder block

2. What are the hardest months for Mrs. Frisby and her children?
    A. November and December
    B. February and March
    C. March and April
    D. January and February

3. Why is Mrs. Frisby depressed when she looks in her pantry?
    A. Water is flooding the pantry.
    B. The food in the pantry is rancid.
    C. There is no food in the pantry.
    D. She is tired of feeding her children the same food every day.

4. Where does Mrs. Frisby find the corn, nuts, and mushrooms?
    A. In a hole in the ground
    B. In a field
    C. Under the farm house
    D. In a hollow tree stump

5. Which of these is a symptom of Timothy's illness?
    A. Muscle aches
    B. Stomach pain
    C. Shortness of breath
    D. Sneezing

6. Mrs. Frisby worries about all of the following on her trip to Mr. Ages EXCEPT:
   A. The farmer's cat
   B. The sun going down
   C. The farmer's dog
   D. The long, risky journey

7. From what does Mr. Ages make his draughts and powders?
   A. Seeds, stalks, and pods from weeds and other plants
   B. Chemicals in his laboratory
   C. Minerals found around his home
   D. Berries and fruits

8. Mr. Ages had treated Timothy previously. For what was Timothy treated?
   A. Timothy had been stung by a wasp.
   B. Timothy had fallen and broken his leg.
   C. Timothy had been bitten by a poisonous spider.
   D. Timothy had been bitten by a poisonous snake.

9. What does Mr. Ages's house resemble?
   A. The home of a hermit
   B. Mrs. Frisby's home
   C. The home of a tree frog
   D. The home of a raccoon

10. What illness does Timothy have?
    A. Food poisoning
    B. Influenza
    C. Cholera
    D. Pneumonia

Assignment 2
The Crow and the Cat, Mr. Fitzgibbon's Plow, & Five Days

1. Which phrase does NOT describe Dragon?
    - A. Mouth full of curving fangs
    - B. Green eyes
    - C. Orange and white in color
    - D. Seven claws on each foot

2. Identify Jeremy.
    - A. Farmer Fitzgiggon's cat
    - B. Mrs. Frisby's son
    - C. Farmer Fitzgibbons's dog
    - D. The crow who befriends Mrs. Frisby

3. Who says that the size of an animal's brain is no measure of its capacity?
    - A. The Lady Shrew
    - B. Mrs. Frisby
    - C. Jeremy
    - D. Mr. Frisby

4. What upcoming event forces Mrs. Frisby to take risks and seek help?
    - A. Moving Day
    - B. The first day of spring
    - C. Harvesting Day
    - D. Timothy's birthday

5. Why must all the animals move out of the garden when winter is over?
    - A. Farmer Fitzgibbon's plow will run over them if they stay.
    - B. There is no shade for protection from the sun in the garden.
    - C. They could be washed away in the spring rains.
    - D. The powders, fertilizers, and sprays used in the garden make the animals sick if they stay.

6. Why didn't the Frisbys make their winter home in the barn lofts or attics like some field mice?
   A. The garden had been the winter home of the Frisbys for generations; they couldn't give it up.
   B. The Frisbys preferred the relative safety and freedom of the outdoors.
   C. The Frisbys didn't know about the lofts and attics.
   D. There wasn't enough room in the barn lofts and attics for all of the animals.

7. Why is the thawing frost a problem for the Frisbys?
   A. It means plowing day will soon come and their safety will be in jeopardy.
   B. It makes their home cold and damp.
   C. It fills their home with mud.
   D. It means the cat will be coming more often.

8. Why does Mr. Fitzgibbon have to wait an extra five days to plow?
   A. He needs to order a new linch pin from Hendersons.
   B. He has to wait for a new tractor tire to come in.
   C. Mr. Henderson is busy and can't come by to fix the tractor for a few days.
   D. The plow needs a new blade.

9. After Mrs. Frisby runs from Dragon and climbs the dead asparagus plant, what does she see beyond the cat?
   A. Rats moving a piece of electrical cable
   B. Timothy trying to follow her
   C. A large pile of corn, nuts, and mushrooms
   D. Farmer Fitzgibbon driving the plow towards the garden

Assignment 3
A Favor from Jeremy, The Owl, & "Go to the Rats"

1. Who is the oldest animal in the forest?
    A. The fox
    B. Jeremy
    C. The bear
    D. The owl

2. What convinces Mrs. Frisby to go see the owl?
    A. The sun warms her, and she knows the frost will soon be gone.
    B. She remembered that Mr. Frisby used to say, "Nothing ventured, nothing gained."
    C. She thinks of Timothy and the big plow blade.
    D. She sees Dragon lurking nearby.

3. What is the best time to see the owl?
    A. Noon
    B. Dawn
    C. Dusk
    D. Early afternoon

4. Why is Timothy not told his mother is going to see the owl?
    A. It would be bad luck to talk about Mrs. Frisby's mission until it is complete.
    B. He is sleeping the whole time.
    C. He is delirious and wouldn't understand anyway.
    D. They don't want him to worry or feel responsible for the risk his mother is taking.

5. Why does Mrs. Frisby hesitate before going into the owl's house?
    A. She thinks the owl might eat her.
    B. She thinks Jeremy might leave her.
    C. It is too dark.
    D. The floor is uneven.

6. What is the owl's advice to Mrs. Frisby?
    A. To go home and stop bothering him
    B. To take a chance on moving Timothy to the house of her nearest relative
    C. To go see the rat Nicodemus
    D. To leave before he eats her

7. What does "in the lee" mean?
    A. Having plenty of what one needs
    B. Going a good way; following a good course of action
    C. In trouble
    D. On the calm side, the side the wind does not blow from

Assignment 4
In the Rosebush, Brutus, & In the Library

1. How does Timothy know that Moving Day is near?
    A. He overhears Mrs. Frisby talking to the other children.
    B. He sneaks outside and sees that the weather is warm.
    C. He overhears Martin talking with Cynthia.
    D. He smells the melting frost.

2. Why doesn't Dragon follow animals into the rose bush?
    A. Mrs. Fitzgibbon will beat him if she sees him in the bush.
    B. He is afraid of it.
    C. The thorns deter him.
    D. Following the animals into the bush would be too undignified.

3. What happens when Mrs. Frisby pushes the branch on the rose bush?
    A. It opens like a swinging door.
    B. It pushes back.
    C. She gets a thorn stuck in her hand.
    D. She sees Dragon behind it.

4. Mrs. Frisby encounters someone she knows in the rose bush. Who?
    A. Mr. Ages
    B. Farmer Fitzgibbon
    C. Jeremy
    D. Dragon

5. Which phrase does NOT describe Justin?
    A. Dark gray in color
    B. Alert
    C. Bigger than Brutus
    D. Handsome

6. Mrs. Frisby is astonished by many things in the corridor of the rat hole. Which of these is NOT something that astonished her?
    A. Green, blue, and yellow glass
    B. Speakers playing music
    C. Recessed lighting
    D. Carpeting

7. When do the rats collect the lights they use?
    A. Around New Years Day
    B. Before Christmas
    C. Christmas Day
    D. During the summer

8. Which is NOT something Mrs. Frisby notices about Nicodemus when she meets him?
    A. He has a patch of black fur on his right ear.
    B. He carries a satchel.
    C. He has a scar on his face.
    D. His left eye has a patch over it.

9. Where does Justin take Mrs. Frisby to wait until the meeting finishes?
    A. The laboratory
    B. The holding cell
    C. The atrium
    D. The library

Assignment 5
Isabella, A Powder for Dragon, & The Marketplace

1. Why does Mrs. Frisby decide against leaving the library to look around?
    A. She was afraid she would get lost.
    B. She sees Justin watching the library door from down the hall.
    C. Nicodemus told her to wait in the library. She doesn't want to pry; she is there for help.
    D. The library doors were too heavy for her to push open. She decided to give up trying to open them.

2. Who or what does Isabella think Mrs. Frisby is?
    A. An inspector
    B. An imposter
    C. A spy from the outside or from NIMH
    D. A thief trying to steal some of their provisions

3. What does Mrs. Frisby learn from Isabella about the rat colony?
    A. They are plotting against Dragon.
    B. They are ill.
    C. Jenner did not like the Plan and deserted.
    D. They are building a new home in the forest.

4. What does Nicodemus call Arthur?
    A. The chief of police
    B. The captain of the guard
    C. The chief engineer
    D. The chief of the fire department

5. What does Nicodemus take from his satchel to help him see?
    A. A pair of glasses
    B. A reading glass
    C. Bifocals
    D. Binoculars

6. According to Nicodemus, what did the owl mean by moving Mrs. Frisby's house "in the lee" of the stone?
   A. The house should be in a carved-out area of the stone.
   B. The house should be on top of the stone where Mrs. Frisby can see the plow coming.
   C. The house should be in close behind the rock where the plow does not reach.
   D. The house should be under the rock.

7. According to Justin, what do the rats do to Dragon when they have a long project?
   A. Tie him up
   B. Lock him in the shed
   C. Lull him to sleep with music from the radio
   D. Put sleeping powder in his food

8. Who usually gets Dragon out of the rats' way?
   A. Justin
   B. Brutus
   C. Nicodemus
   D. Mr. Ages

9. What object in Nicodemus's office particularly catches Mrs. Frisby's attention?
   A. A painting of NIMH
   B. The radio
   C. A snow globe
   D. A picture of Jonathan

10. With whom does Nicodemus usually go to the market?
    A. Mr. Ages and Justin
    B. His older brother Gerald and his friend Jenner
    C. His older brother Jenner and his friend Gerald
    D. His younger brother Justin and his friend Gerald

Assignment 6
In the Cage & The Maze

1. According to the man, why were they able to catch the rats?
    A. The rats were distracted.
    B. The rats had grown careless.
    C. The rats were sleeping.
    D. The rats were too tired to run away.

2. Where do the men take Nicodemus, Jenner, and the other rats?
    A. To a warehouse
    B. To a laboratory
    C. To the farm
    D. To a pet store

3. Which is NOT a reason given as to why Nicodemus dislikes his cage so much?
    A. It is filthy from other rats being in there before him.
    B. It is too small; he can only move three hops forward and back again.
    C. He hates the feeling he is at the mercy of someone he does not know.
    D. The mere fact that it is a cage makes it horrible.

4. According to Nicodemus, what do the rats eventually learn after their initial fear and uncertainty after their capture?
    A. Uncertainty is the worst thing they will undergo.
    B. The men are trying to get the rats to fight among themselves.
    C. Their worst fears will be confirmed; they will all die.
    D. Cats are allowed in the room at night, to guard the cages.

5. How are the rats in Group C different from A and B?
    A. They receive injections of the "smart" serum.
    B. They are the older rats.
    C. They are the control group; they receive no injections.
    D. They are the youngest rats.

6. According to Nicodemus, why does Dr. Schultz keep the rats in captivity?
    A. To test new kinds of rat food
    B. To test a serum and see if it makes them smarter
    C. To breed more rats
    D. To observe how rats behave in captivity

7. What happens if Nicodemus goes down the wrong corridor in the Maze?
    A. He gets squirted with water.
    B. He gets an electric shock through the floor.
    C. George picks him up.
    D. He does not get a treat from George.

8. As Nicodemus runs through the Maze more often, what happens to his time?
    A. It remains the same.
    B. It gets shorter.
    C. It gets longer.
    D. It varies, sometimes it is long, sometimes it is shorter.

9. What other test does Nicodemus describe, besides the Maze?
    A. Hearing test
    B. Vision test
    C. Shape recognition test
    D. IQ test

10. Who escapes from Julie to look around the laboratory?
    A. Justin
    B. Jenner
    C. Jonathan
    D. Nicodemus

Assignment 7
A Lesson in Reading & The Air Ducts

1. What were the injections doing to Group A?
    A. The rats were becoming smarter and stopped aging.
    B. The injections were slowly killing them.
    C. The rats were becoming fatter and stronger.
    D. The rats were becoming better listeners.

2. What were Dr. Schultz and his assistants attempting to do when they showed the rats a picture of a rat and symbols while playing a recording that said "Are, Aie, Tea, Rat"?
    A. They were teaching the rats nonsense words.
    B. They were teaching the rats to listen.
    C. They were teaching the rats to read.
    D. They were teaching the rats to sing.

3. How did Justin get out of his cage after the doctor and his assistants went home for the night?
    A. Jenner helped him open the cage door.
    B. His cage door had not been closed properly.
    C. Nicodemus helped him open the cage door.
    D. He read the instructions on the bottom of the cage.

4. Which of the following is NOT a reason Justin didn't want Nicodemus to explore the laboratory with him?
    A. Nicodemus was sleeping, and Justin didn't want to disturb him.
    B. Justin thought if the two of them got caught the doctors would know how smart the rats had become.
    C. Justin was being cautious.
    D. Justin didn't want Nicodemus to get into trouble.

5. Why did the rats steal a spool of thread to help them explore the ducts?
    A. They used it as a bridge over vent holes.
    B. They needed it as a rope to help them climb into the ducts.
    C. They needed it to tie up the cat.
    D. They used it to help them keep from getting lost.

6. What does Jonathan the mouse ask Nicodemus to do for the mice?
    A. Jonathan asks Nicodemus for directions through the air ducts.
    B. Jonathan asks Nicodemus exactly where they are going.
    C. Jonathan wants to know how to open his cage.
    D. Jonathan asks Nicodemus to open the cages of the mice and help them escape.

7. What does Nicodemus decide regarding the mice?
    A. To allow the mice to follow the rats through the air duct
    B. To teach the mice how to open their cages
    C. To leave them a spool of thread of their own
    D. To leave the mice in the laboratory

8. Which of the following is NOT one of Jenner's concerns regarding what the rats would do after they escaped?
    A. He didn't want them to live in sewer pipes and eat garbage.
    B. He was concerned about where they would go.
    C. He was worried about how they would defend themselves.
    D. He was concerned that the rats wouldn't fit in with other rats.

9. What happens to six of the eight mice in the air duct?
    A. They fall through an air vent.
    B. They become ill.
    C. They get lost.
    D. They are blown away.

10. How did the mice help save the rats?
    A. They figured out how to open the locked screen.
    B. They kept the rats from blowing away.
    C. They gnawed through the wires controlling the air.
    D. They found a wire the rats could use as a bridge over an air vent hole.

Assignment 8
The Boniface Estate, The Main Hall, & The Toy Tinker

1. Which of the following is NOT a way the rats know the Boniface Estate is deserted before entering the house?
    A. There is a padlock on the fence.
    B. There is no garbage in the trash can.
    C. Lights come on even though no one is standing near a lamp.
    D. There are weeds growing in front of the entrance gate.

2. How did the rats keep themselves from being detected by the caretaker-gardener?
    A. They were careful to only go in places the gardener-caretaker would not see.
    B. They made the mice do the house cleaning.
    C. They took out the trash and cleaned up after themselves.
    D. They learned how to use a vacuum.

3. What did the rats do late into the night all winter long while staying at the Boniface Estate?
    A. The rats played games like the old days before NIMH.
    B. The rats learned to cook.
    C. The rats studied books and practiced writing.
    D. The rats built machines.

4. What does Justin show Mrs. Frisby when she returns to the rosebush in the late afternoon?
    A. The workshop
    B. The garage
    C. The library
    D. The kitchen

5. What is "The Plan"?
    A. To live without stealing
    B. To live without fear
    C. To live exactly as people do
    D. To live without fighting

6. What is the difference between the evolution of rats and monkeys according to one of the books that Nicodemus read?
   A. Rats were once more advanced than any other animals but their lives were too easy and they got lazy. Monkeys had to fight for survival, so they evolved faster.
   B. Rats had smaller brains and therefore evolved much more slowly than the monkeys.
   C. Because rats had more natural predators, their life spans were much shorter than the life spans of the monkeys. They didn't have as much time to learn and evolve.
   D. The rats' lives were very difficult, and it kept them from evolving further.

7. The rats read many books while staying at the Boniface house. What kind of books were difficult to find?
   A. Books about evolution
   B. Books about electricity
   C. Books about rats
   D. Books about civilization

8. Why are rats the most hated animals on earth, according to Nicodemus?
   A. They carry diseases.
   B. They steal.
   C. They are filthy.
   D. They look evil.

9. After they left the Boniface Estate, where did the rats want their new home to be? Why?
   A. Near a city for supplies
   B. Near fresh water so they wouldn't have to carry water far
   C. Near a hill so they could watch for the people from NIMH who might come after them
   D. Near mountains because of the natural caves

10. How did the Toy Tinker die?
    A. Fell and hit his head
    B. Old age
    C. A heart attack
    D. Accidental electrocution

Assignment 9
Thorn Valley & Captured

1. Describe what Nicodemus and the rats found in the Toy Tinker's truck.
    A. Mechanical rats
    B. Tools small enough for the rats to use
    C. A huge stash of food
    D. A box with NIMH printed on the side

2. How did the rats get running water and electricity?
    A. They hooked into the city supply.
    B. They made an electrical generator and pumped water from a nearby stream.
    C. They stole it from Farmer Fitzgibbon's supply.
    D. They caught the rain water up high in a big barrel and used the natural downward flow of the water to turn the wheel of an electrical generator.

3. What is a "rat race"?
    A. A laboratory test where two rats are put in the same maze to see which one is smarter
    B. A race in which the participants are required to stop at various check points to pick up items
    C. A race in which the participants run the same course over and over again trying to better their times
    D. A race in which no matter how fast you run, you don't get anywhere

4. What is the result of Mrs. Jones's purchasing a vacuum?
    A. Dragon spends more time outdoors.
    B. Several mice are sucked into it and killed.
    C. The rats suffer an electrical shortage.
    D. The electric company builds a new plant and causes more pollution.

5. How did Nicodemus become acquainted with the owl?
    A. He encountered the owl while trying out his flying machine.
    B. The owl caught him for dinner.
    C. A chipmunk suggested Nicodemus should go see the owl.
    D. Mrs. Frisby told him about the owl.

6. Why do Nicodemus and most of the other rats want to leave their current location and start over?
   A. They didn't want to steal any longer.
   B. They were afraid of getting caught or discovered in their current location.
   C. Farmer Fitzgibbon was clearing brush, coming dangerously close to the rose bush.
   D. Life had become too easy; they wanted more of a challenge.

7. Why didn't Jonathan Frisby tell his wife about NIMH?
   A. He didn't want to take a chance on hurting her with the news.
   B. He was sworn to secrecy.
   C. He didn't want her to think he was abnormal or freakish.
   D. He didn't see any point in telling her since it couldn't be changed.

8. What happened to Jenner?
   A. He was accidentally electrocuted.
   B. He was killed while putting sleeping powder in Dragon's dish.
   C. He left with some others who were against The Plan.
   D. He left to go supervise and help the mice.

9. Why do the rats want to destroy the machinery and the other conveniences of their current home?
   A. They regret having made it.
   B. They don't want it to be discovered.
   C. They don't want other animals to use it.
   D. It was all made with stolen materials.

10. What happens to Mrs. Frisby after she puts the sleeping draught into Dragon's bowl?
    A. Dragon chases her, and she gets lost.
    B. She realizes Mrs. Fitzgibbon has unknowingly blocked her exit, and she has nowhere to go.
    C. Billy Fitzgibbon traps her under a colander.
    D. She becomes very sleepy and realizes she has inhaled too much of the dusty powder.

Assignment 10
Seven Dead Rats & Escape

1. Who is Porgy?
    - A. The Fitzgibbons' former canary
    - B. The Fitzgibbons' pig
    - C. The Fitzgibbons' cat
    - D. The Fitzgibbons' dog

2. What does Paul try to convince Billy to do, and what is his argument?
    - A. Release Mrs. Frisby because she's a wild animal and shouldn't be kept in a cage.
    - B. Put Mrs. Frisby in a box because he's afraid of rats and doesn't want to see her.
    - C. Kill Mrs. Frisby so she won't have babies and increase the number of rats on the farm.
    - D. Release Mrs. Frisby from the cage because she's a disgusting rodent who shouldn't be kept indoors.

3. What happened at Henderson's Hardware Store?
    - A. Mr. Henderson found mice stealing a motor.
    - B. Six or seven rats were electrocuted.
    - C. Mr. Henderson had a heart attack.
    - D. Mr. Henderson killed six or seven rats he found in the store.

4. Why did the federal government send a squad with a truckload of equipment to the hardware store?
    - A. Mr. Henderson called them to help get rid of the rats.
    - B. Mr. Henderson found the dead rats and rat droppings, and he wanted his shop decontaminated to make sure it was safe for himself and his customers.
    - C. The truck was filled with various pieces of equipment that needed parts for repair. The squad was sent to the hardware store to get parts and ask for Mr. Henderson's help in repairing the equipment.
    - D. Fred Smith had written an article entitled "Mechanized Rats Invade Hardware Store," and they suspected the rats were those missing from the lab.

5. Why do Paul and Mr. Fitzgibbon believe the Public Health Service is so concerned about the rats?
    - A. They think the rats escaped from a lab.
    - B. They think the rats have rabies.
    - C. They think the rats have special super powers.
    - D. They think the rats are carrying diptheria.

6. Why doesn't Justin simply open the door of Mrs. Frisby's cage?
    A. He can't reach it.
    B. He can't; he isn't physically strong enough.
    C. He doesn't want Mr. Fitzgibbons to become suspicious.
    D. Dragon is sitting in front of it.

7. Why does Justin believe Mrs. Frisby has brought the rats good luck?
    A. Her husband, Johnathan, had always been a positive influence for the rats; now she seems to have taken his place.
    B. She warns the rats about the exterminators who were coming to poison them.
    C. Although the rats have been getting into difficulties, Mrs. Frisby always seems to come through with a good idea to help.
    D. Since she came to the rats, The Plan has been executed flawlessly.

8. Who does Justin believe the seven dead rats are?
    A. Jenner and his friends
    B. The Group B rats from the lab
    C. Jonathan, Jenner, and other rats they have rounded up
    D. Ordinary rats

9. What is the problem the rats encounter while trying to move Mrs. Frisby's house?
    A. The shrew won't let the rats move Mrs. Frisby's house.
    B. The children are scared of the rats and won't come out of the house.
    C. Jeremy won't let the rats move Mrs. Frisby's house.
    D. Timothy is too sick to move.

10. Which of the following is something the rats did in order to move Mrs. Frisby's house?
    A. They "jacked it up" to get wheels under it.
    B. They made a crane to move the stone.
    C. They used simple machines.
    D. They formed a "bucket brigade" to move the belongings.

Assignment 11
At the Meeting, The Doctor, & Epilogue

1. Why does Brutus come to find Mrs. Frisby?
    A. Isabella misses her.
    B. Nicodemus wants to see her.
    C. Justin wants to see her.
    D. Mr. Ages wants to see her.

2. Who does Nicodemus believe is coming to get the rats?
    A. Exterminators
    B. Farmer Fitzgibbon
    C. Men from NIMH
    D. Men from the city government

3. What did the rats do to make the exterminators believe it was an ordinary rat hole?
    A. They invited ordinary rats to act as decoys.
    B. They burned all the evidence of an advanced civilization.
    C. They gnawed through all the carpet, water pipes, and electric wires.
    D. They moved all the equipment to the cave and brought in garbage.

4. Why is Mrs. Frisby concerned that only seven rats exited the cave at first?
    A. She couldn't understand where the other 143 rats had gone.
    B. Dragon was nearby, and she feared for their lives.
    C. She feared they would be caught by the exterminators.
    D. Three rats were missing, and she feared they were dead.

5. What do the seven rats do to trick the exterminators?
    A. They travel through their secret tunnel to the cave.
    B. They gnaw through the tube pumping cyanide into the hole.
    C. They pretend to be dead.
    D. They run out in groups making it look like dozens of rats are exiting the hole.

6. Who was the eighth rat that left the rat hole and fell unconscious?
   A. Brutus
   B. Isabella
   C. Nicodemus
   D. Justin

7. Who do the children believe went back into the hole to save the rat who had fallen?
   A. Justin
   B. Brutus
   C. Jonathan
   D. Nicodemus

8. Where do the Frisbys live in the summer?
   A. Thorn Valley
   B. Near a brook
   C. With the rats
   D. In a natural cave

9. Why does Mrs. Frisby decide to tell the children about NIMH?
   A. She believes they have a right to know because they might be different from other mice.
   B. Nicodemus told her to do so.
   C. She thought it would make a good bedtime story.
   D. She can't keep a secret.

10. What does Martin want to do in the fall? Why?
    A. Visit the rats with Jeremy's help
    B. Get a job so he can be more helpful to his mother
    C. Visit NIMH so he can have the same injections as his father
    D. Move to Thorn Valley permanently

ANSWER KEY: STUDY QUESTIONS *Mrs. Frisby And The Rats Of NIMH*

	1	2	3	4	5	6	7	8	9	10	11
1	C	B	D	D	C	B	A	B	B	A	B
2	D	D	C	C	C	B	C	C	C	A	C
3	D	D	C	A	C	A	D	C	D	B	D
4	D	A	D	A	C	A	A	A	D	D	D
5	C	A	A	C	B	C	D	A	C	B	D
6	A	B	C	B	C	B	D	A	A	C	A
7	A	A	D	A	D	B	A	C	A	B	A
8	C	A		A	D	B	C	B	C	A	B
9	A	A		D	B	C	D	D	B	A	A
10	D				B	A	A	C	C	C	A

VOCABULARY WORKSHEETS

VOCABULARY ASSIGNMENT 1 *Mrs. Frisby And The Rats Of NIMH*

Part I: Using Prior Knowledge and Contextual Clues

Below are the sentences in which the vocabulary words appear in the text. Read the sentence. Use any clues you can find in the sentence combined with your prior knowledge, and write what you think the underlined words mean on the lines provided.

1. It was a winter house, such as some field mice move to when food becomes <u>scarce</u>, and the living too hard in the woods and pastures.

   _____

2. The bedroom, formed by the second oval, was warm but dark, even at <u>midday</u>.

   _____

3. She could see from the light <u>filtering</u> down the entrance tunnel that the sun was up.

   _____

4. In the stump there was a hole, and out of the hole <u>protruded</u> something that looked like a leaf, but was not.

   _____

5. "Two weeks," said Martin <u>authoritatively</u>.

   _____

6. But since that would have led her close to the farmhouse and the barn . . . she had to plot a much more <u>roundabout</u> way, circling the whole wide farmyard.

   _____

7. From that time on he tended to stumble a little when he walked, especially when he was tired; he never grew as big or as <u>vigorous</u> as his brother Martin.

   _____

8. Mr. Ages's house, somewhat larger than a shoebox but about the same shape, resembled the house of a <u>hermit</u>.

   _____

9. "So high that he feels burning hot to the touch, runs with <u>perspiration</u>, and yet he shivers with cold at the same time."

   _____

10. There were harsher plants as well-spiked jimson weeds and poisonous dark pokeberries, and bees <u>droning</u> everywhere.

    _____

Mrs. Frisby And The Rats Of NIMH Vocabulary Worksheet Assignment 1 Continued

Part II: Determining the Meaning -- Match the vocabulary words to their dictionary definitions.

____ 1.	SCARCE	A.	Any person living in seclusion
____ 2.	MIDDAY	B.	Insufficient to satisfy the need or demand
____ 3.	FILTERING	C.	Making a continuous, low, monotonous sound
____ 4.	PROTRUDED	D.	The middle of the day; noon
____ 5.	AUTHORITATIVELY	E.	Slipping through slowly as if through an obstruction
____ 6.	ROUNDABOUT	F.	Strong; active; robust
____ 7.	VIGOROUS	G.	Sweat
____ 8.	HERMIT	H.	Stuck out; extended beyond
____ 9.	PERSPIRATION	I.	In a commanding way
____ 10.	DRONING	J.	Circuitous or indirect

VOCABULARY ASSIGNMENT 2 *Mrs. Frisby And The Rats Of NIMH*

Part I: Using Prior Knowledge and Contextual Clues

Below are the sentences in which the vocabulary words appear in the text. Read the sentence. Use any clues you can find in the sentence combined with your prior knowledge, and write what you think the underlined words mean on the lines provided.

1. She could go home by the same roundabout way she had come, in which case she would surely end up walking alone in the woods in the dark-- a frightening prospect, for at night the forest was alive with danger.

   _____

2. When at length she came abreast of the barn, she saw the cattle wire fence that marked the other end of the pasture; and as she approached it, she was startled by a sudden outburst of noise.

   _____

3. As she watched, he fluttered to the top of the fence, where he perched nervously for a moment.

   _____

4. It was twined and twisted and twined again around his right ankle, and she saw she would have to cut through it three times to get it off.

   _____

5. However, she thought it wise not to say so, under those circumstances.

   _____

6. When Mrs. Frisby went into her house, she found Timothy asleep and the other children waiting, frightened, sad, and subdued.

   _____

7. The remark was illogical, of course, for they both knew that without Mr. Fitzgibbon's plow there would be no garden at all, and there was no way he could turn the earth without also turning up their houses.

   _____

8. Some find their way to barn lofts; some even creep into people's houses and live under eaves or in attics, taking their chances with mousetraps.

   _____

9. Mr. Fitzgibbon had backed the tractor out of the big, cluttered shed where he kept it.

   _____

10. Five days, although a respite, was too short.

    _____

Mrs. Frisby And The Rats Of NIMH Vocabulary Worksheet Assignment 2 Continued

Part II: Determining the Meaning -- Match the vocabulary words to their dictionary definitions.

____ 1. PROSPECT   A. Quieted; less active than usual

____ 2. ABREAST   B. Contrary to or disregarding the rules of logic

____ 3. FLUTTERED   C. A break

____ 4. TWINED   D. Conditions surrounding an event

____ 5. CIRCUMSTANCES   E. Interwoven; wrapped around

____ 6. SUBDUED   F. Side by side; beside each other in a line

____ 7. ILLOGICAL   G. Overhanging, lower edges of a roof

____ 8. EAVES   H. Containing too many things, and often unorganized

____ 9. CLUTTERED   I. Outlook for the future

____ 10. RESPITE   J. Waved or flapped about

VOCABULARY ASSIGNMENT 3 *Mrs. Frisby And The Rats Of NIMH*

Part I: Using Prior Knowledge and Contextual Clues

Below are the sentences in which the vocabulary words appear in the text. Read the sentence. Use any clues you can find in the sentence combined with your prior knowledge, and write what you think the underlined words mean on the lines provided.

1. So he clucked <u>sympathetically</u> when he heard Mrs. Frisby's story, cocked his head to one side, and thought as hard as he could for as long as he could, which was about thirty seconds.

   _____

2. Mrs. Frisby <u>hesitated</u>. It was one thing to jump on a crow's back when the cat is only three jumps away and coming fast, but quite another to do it deliberately, and to fly deep into a dark and unknown forest.

   _____

3. It was one thing to jump on a crow's back when the cat is only three jumps away and coming fast, but quite another to do it <u>deliberately</u>, and to fly deep into a dark and unknown forest.

   _____

4. The time to see him is just at <u>dusk</u>. Then, when the light gets dim, he comes to the entrance of the hollow and watches while the dark comes in.

   _____

5. Timothy was down below, taking a nap, and had not been told about the <u>expedition</u> lest he worry and blame himself for the risk his mother must take

   _____

6. But Jeremy suddenly saw that she was <u>trembling</u> and realized that she must be afraid.

   _____

7. So smooth was the motion that they seemed to stand still, and Mrs. Frisby <u>ventured</u> to open her eyes and lift her head just a trifle.

   _____

8. When she opened them, the garden patch had vanished far behind them, and Jeremy, searching the trees below, began a long, slanting <u>descent</u>.

   _____

9. Indeed, he gave an <u>agitated</u> flutter of his wings and half flew, half hopped closer to her, bending forward until his great sharp beak was only a few inches from her face.

   _____

10. Mrs. Frisby was close to complete <u>bewilderment</u>.

    _____

Mrs. Frisby And The Rats Of NIMH Vocabulary Worksheet Assignment 3 Continued

Part II: Determining the Meaning -- Match the vocabulary words to their dictionary definitions.

____ 1. SYMPATHETICALLY   A. Was reluctant or waited to act because of fear or indecision

____ 2. HESITATED   B. In a way showing agreement in feeling

____ 3. DELIBERATELY   C. Journey or voyage made for a specific purpose

____ 4. DUSK   D. Shaking involuntarily with quick, short movements as from fear, excitement, or cold

____ 5. EXPEDITION   E. Troubled or nervous

____ 6. TREMBLING   F. The condition of being completely puzzled

____ 7. VENTURED   G. The moving from a higher to a lower place

____ 8. DESCENT   H. Intentionally; on purpose; with forethought

____ 9. AGITATED   I. Period of partial darkness between day and night as the sun begins to set

____ 10. BEWILDERMENT   J. Dared to do something dangerous or risky

VOCABULARY ASSIGNMENT 4 *Mrs. Frisby And The Rats Of NIMH*

Part I: Using Prior Knowledge and Contextual Clues

Below are the sentences in which the vocabulary words appear in the text. Read the sentence. Use any clues you can find in the sentence combined with your prior knowledge, and write what you think the underlined words mean on the lines provided.

1. Coming silently down the tunnel, she could hear them talking in the room below, and she paused a moment to <u>eavesdrop</u> on their conversation.

   _____

2. The branch <u>yielded</u> easily, rather like a swinging door, and behind it she saw a trail, a sort of tunnel through the bush, wide enough so that she could walk into it without touching thorns on either side.

   _____

3. She felt like crying-- after coming all this way, after flying to see the owl, to be turned back so <u>abruptly</u> at the end.

   _____

4. He sounded <u>cordial</u> enough, but he was startled.

   _____

5. Brutus now looked <u>astonished</u>. "You both know her? Who is she?"

   _____

6. "It was temporarily <u>adjourned</u>," said Justin, "to wait for you."

   _____

7. The light came from the walls, where every foot or so on both sides a tiny light bulb had been <u>recessed</u> and the hole in which it stood, like a small window, had been covered with a square of colored glass-- blue, green, or yellow.

   _____

8. They continued along the <u>corridor</u>, which curved always slightly to the right, so Mrs. Frisby could never really tell how long it was, and which soon began to incline more steeply into the ground.

   _____

9. They continued along the corridor, which curved always slightly to the right, so Mrs. Frisby could never really tell how long it was, and which soon began to <u>incline</u> more steeply into the ground.

   _____

10. It went down in a spiral and each step was neatly <u>inlaid</u> with a rectangular piece of slate.

    _____

Mrs. Frisby And The Rats Of NIMH Vocabulary Worksheet Assignment 4 Continued

Part II: Determining the Meaning -- Match the vocabulary words to their dictionary definitions.

____ 1. EAVESDROP   A. Set back

____ 2. YIELDED   B. Passageway giving access to rooms, apartments, etc.

____ 3. ABRUPTLY   C. Listen secretly to a private conversaion

____ 4. CORDIAL   D. Suspended (a meeting) until a later time or to another place

____ 5. ASTONISHED   E. Courteous; gracious; friendly

____ 6. ADJOURNED   F. Mounted into and flush with the surface of an object

____ 7. RECESSED   G. Suddenly or unexpectedly

____ 8. CORRIDOR   H. Slant upward

____ 9. INCLINE   I. Gave way

____ 10. INLAID   J. Filled with sudden, overpowering surprise or wonder

VOCABULARY ASSIGNMENT 5 *Mrs. Frisby And The Rats Of NIMH*

Part I: Using Prior Knowledge and Contextual Clues

Below are the sentences in which the vocabulary words appear in the text. Read the sentence. Use any clues you can find in the sentence combined with your prior knowledge, and write what you think the underlined words mean on the lines provided.

1. Mrs. Frisby started all this, trying to make head or tail of it, but she could not. It was quite incomprehensible.

   _____

2. The girl rat, her alarm apparently subsiding, began picking up her scattered papers.

   _____

3. "I guess your not a spy," said the girl-rat. She sounded mildly disappointed. Then she added irrelevantly: "Justin's not married."

   _____

4. The strange rate was named Arthur. He was stocky, square and muscular, with bright, hard eyes.

   _____

5. Nicodemus took the reading glass from his satchel, opened it, and through it gravely examined Mrs. Frisby's face.

   _____

6. Nicodemus took the reading glass from his satchel, opened it, and through it gravely examined Mrs. Frisby's face.

   _____

7. They had tied it on tope of the harrow for weight, and it fell off just as they were finishing the garden.

   _____

8. "You did it yesterday!" cried Mrs. Frisby, remembering the figures toiling the wire through the grass, remembering how strangely disinterested Dragon had seemed when he saw her.

   _____

9. The room she entered was smaller than the library, but much more comfortably-- almost elegantly--furnished

   _____

10. As we walked, we were joined by more rats; at that time of day they converged on the marketplace from all directions.

    _____

Mrs. Frisby And The Rats Of NIMH Vocabulary Worksheet Assignment 5 Continued

Part II: Determining the Meaning -- Match the vocabulary words to their dictionary definitions.

____ 1.	INCOMPREHENSIBLE	A.	In a splendid or luxurious style or design
____ 2.	SUBSIDING	B.	Becoming quieter or less active
____ 3.	IRRELEVANTLY	C.	Small bag, sometimes with a shoulder strap
____ 4.	STOCKY	D.	Seriously; solemnly
____ 5.	GRAVELY	E.	Came together to meet at a point or in a line
____ 6.	SATCHEL	F.	Impossible to understand
____ 7.	HARROW	G.	Working with exhausting labor or effort
____ 8.	TOILING	H.	Having a sturdy form or build
____ 9.	ELEGANTLY	I.	Agricultural implement with spike-like teeth or upright disks, for leveling and breaking-up clods in plowed land
____ 10.	CONVERGED	J.	In a manner not having anything to do with the matter at hand

VOCABULARY ASSIGNMENT 6 *Mrs. Frisby And The Rats Of NIMH*

Part I: Using Prior Knowledge and Contextual Clues

Below are the sentences in which the vocabulary words appear in the text. Read the sentence. Use any clues you can find in the sentence combined with your prior knowledge, and write what you think the underlined words mean on the lines provided.

1. And yet you could hardly even call it stealing--it was waste food, and all they did with it was haul it away to the city <u>incinerator</u>.

   _____

2. No, I was firmly and <u>inextricably</u> caught, snared in the net and helpless.

   _____

3. A few of the rats snarled and tried to bite; I did not, and neither did Jenner; it was too obviously <u>futile</u>.

   _____

4. But our end held only rows of cages on shelves, each with a tag on it, and each separated from its neighbors by wooden <u>partitions</u> on both sides.

   _____

5. And we were always well fed, though the food, scientifically <u>compiled</u> pellets, was not what you'd call delicious.

   _____

6. During the days that followed, our lives fell into a pattern, and the reason for our <u>captivity</u> gradually became clear.

   _____

7. When you lived in a cage, you can't bear not to run, even if what you're running toward is an <u>illusion</u>.

   _____

8. It was Julie who opened Justin's cage with a <u>hypodermic</u> in her hand.

   _____

9. I had, after all my running through the corridors, emerged into a trap only a few feet from where I had started, and through a <u>concealed</u> opening up above, George had been watching everything I did.

   _____

10. I had, after all my running through the corridors, <u>emerged</u> into a trap only a few feet from where I had started, and through a concealed opening up above, George had been watching everything I did.

    _____

Mrs. Frisby And The Rats Of NIMH Vocabulary Worksheet Assignment 6 Continued

Part II: Determining the Meaning -- Match the vocabulary words to their dictionary definitions.

____ 1. INCINERATOR   A. In a manner incapable of being disentangled

____ 2. INEXTRICABLY   B. Something that deceives by producing a false impression of reality

____ 3. FUTILE   C. Incapable of producing any result

____ 4. PARTITIONS   D. Syringe or needle that injects medicine under the skin

____ 5. COMPILED   E. Furnace or apparatus for burning materials

____ 6. CAPTIVITY   F. Came forth

____ 7. ILLUSION   G. Made of materials from various sources

____ 8. HYPODERMIC   H. Imprisonment

____ 9. CONCEALED   I. Hidden

____ 10. EMERGED   J. Dividers

VOCABULARY ASSIGNMENT 7 *Mrs. Frisby And The Rats Of NIMH*

Part I: Using Prior Knowledge and Contextual Clues
Below are the sentences in which the vocabulary words appear in the text. Read the sentence. Use any clues you can find in the sentence combined with your prior knowledge, and write what you think the underlined words mean on the lines provided.

1. Mainly he had learned that he could, occasionally at least, jump from his cage and wander around without <u>incurring</u> any anger or injury.

   _____

2. He and the others were preparing a research paper--about us to be published in some scientific journal--so each morning he <u>dictated</u> the results of the previous day's tests into a tape recorder.

   _____

3. But as to what all this was for, none of us had any <u>inkling</u>.

   _____

4. Then if I--if all of us--moved <u>unerringly</u> toward the proper door, he would know we understood the sign.

   _____

5. I should perhaps explain that when Dr. Schultz and the others opened our cages we could never quite see how they did it; they <u>manipulated</u> something under the plastic floor, something we couldn't see.

   _____

6. We were strangers--though as you can imagine, it did not take long for us to develop a feeling of <u>comradeship</u>, for we twenty were alone in a strange world.

   _____

7. Jenner was <u>astute</u> at that sort of thing; he could foresee problems.

   _____

8. It was a clear but <u>plaintive</u> call, the voice of a mouse.

   _____

9. As you can imagine, this caused a certain <u>consternation</u>, coming at the last minute.

   _____

10. In another minute the roar stopped, the rush of air slowed from a <u>gale</u> to a breeze, and we were able to go forward again.

    _____

Mrs. Frisby And The Rats Of NIMH Vocabulary Worksheet Assignment 7 Continued

Part II: Determining the Meaning -- Match the vocabulary words to their dictionary definitions.

____ 1. INCURRING	A.	Worked, operated, or treated with the hands
____ 2. DICTATED	B.	Having or showing a clever or shrewd mind
____ 3. INKLING	C.	Expressing sorrow or melancholy
____ 4. UNERRINGLY	D.	Without mistakes
____ 5. MANIPULATED	E.	A vague idea or notion
____ 6. COMRADESHIP	F.	Bringing upon oneself
____ 7. ASTUTE	G.	Great fear or shock that makes one feel helpless
____ 8. PLAINTIVE	H.	Spoke(n) or read aloud to be written or recorded
____ 9. CONSTERNATION	I.	A very strong wind
____ 10. GALE	J.	Friendship; companionship

VOCABULARY ASSIGNMENT 8 *Mrs. Frisby And The Rats Of NIMH*

Part I: Using Prior Knowledge and Contextual Clues

Below are the sentences in which the vocabulary words appear in the text. Read the sentence. Use any clues you can find in the sentence combined with your prior knowledge, and write what you think the underlined words mean on the lines provided.

1. In the country there were barns and <u>silos</u> stocked with grain and corn, and chicken houses full of eggs.

   _____

2. We had just about decided, after nearly four months of freedom and constant <u>roving</u>, to find a place to settle down--if not permanently, at least for winter.

   _____

3. It was the beginning of a <u>discontent</u> and an idea that kept growing, although slowly.

   _____

4. Oh, there was a caretaker-gardener who came three times a week, and once in a while he would check the house in a <u>cursory</u> sort of way.

   _____

5. Down in the rats home, in the <u>artificial</u> light, it was hard to tell the passage of time.

   _____

6. The children were <u>skeptical</u> at first, then intensely curious, especially Timothy.

   _____

7. That afternoon Mrs. Frisby told the children that she must leave them to <u>confer</u> again with the rats about moving the house.

   _____

8. It was then that the rats were driven to become scavengers and thieves, living on the <u>fringes</u> of a world run by men.

   _____

9. On the map, a big part of it was covered with the <u>contour</u> lines that show mountains.

   _____

10. He was a <u>peddler</u> and mender of toys, the red and gold wagon was his shop and his home, and he had driven into the woods to camp for the night.

    _____

Mrs. Frisby And The Rats Of NIMH Vocabulary Worksheet Assignment 8 Continued

Part II: Determining the Meaning -- Match the vocabulary words to their dictionary definitions.

____ 1.	SILOS	A.	The outline of a figure, mass, land, etc.
____ 2.	ROVING	B.	Have discussions
____ 3.	DISCONTENT	C.	Made by human work or art; not by nature
____ 4.	CURSORY	D.	Doubtful; not easily persuaded or convinced
____ 5.	ARTIFICIAL	E.	Airtight pits or towers in which fodder is stored
____ 6.	SKEPTICAL	F.	Person who goes from place to place selling small articles
____ 7.	CONFER	G.	Dissatisfaction; a restless desire for something more
____ 8.	FRINGES	H.	Performed rapidly with little attention to detail
____ 9.	CONTOUR	I.	Wandering about; going from place to place
____ 10.	PEDDLER	J.	At the outer edge or border

VOCABULARY ASSIGNMENT 9 *Mrs. Frisby And The Rats Of NIMH*

Part I: Using Prior Knowledge and Contextual Clues
Below are the sentences in which the vocabulary words appear in the text. Read the sentence. Use any clues you can find in the sentence combined with your prior knowledge, and write what you think the underlined words mean on the lines provided.

1. But they were silly, fearful creatures; and after looking at me in surprise, they both

   _____

2. Also, we are shorter, so we had little trouble with the spiny underbrush.

   _____

3. He was just more cynical than the rest of us; stealing did not bother him.

   _____

4. And he was a pessimist. He never believed that we could really make it on our own.

   _____

5. We've got seeds; we have our plows; we've cleared and cultivated part of the land near the pond; and in a few days we'll begin our first planting.

   _____

6. We've even dug some irrigation ditches, in case there's a drought.

   _____

7. One, so that if anyone ever finds the cave, there won't be any evidence of what we've been going--nothing but broken bits of metal, debris that will look like ordinary junk.

   _____

8. It was a hole, left for ventilation, and there was a screen over it.

   _____

9. "Don't get panicky, or you'll do something foolish and spoil everything." Thus admonished, she crept forward again until she was near the edge of the cabinet.

   _____

10. Billy, the younger Fitzgibbon son, had been sitting on the kitchen stool, his feet up on the rung, eating berries from a colander.

    _____

Mrs. Frisby And The Rats Of NIMH Vocabulary Worksheet Assignment 9 Continued

Part II: Determining the Meaning -- Match the vocabulary words to their dictionary definitions.

____ 1. SCURRIED   A. Bits and pieces of rubbish; litter

____ 2. SPINY   B. Person who sees everything in a negative or the worst possible way

____ 3. CYNICAL   C. Mildly scolded; spoken to in disapproval

____ 4. PESSIMIST   D. A system that circulates air

____ 5. CULTIVATED   E. Covered with or having thorns or prickles

____ 6. IRRIGATION   F. Means of supplying water via ditches or artificial channels

____ 7. DEBRIS   G. Scampered or ran hastily

____ 8. VENTILATION   H. Strainer; a perforated pan used for draining liquids

____ 9. ADMONISHED   I. Prepared for growing crops

____ 10. COLANDER   J. Believing that people are only motivated by selfishness

VOCABULARY ASSIGNMENT 10 *Mrs. Frisby And The Rats Of NIMH*

Part I: Using Prior Knowledge and Contextual Clues

Below are the sentences in which the vocabulary words appear in the text. Read the sentence. Use any clues you can find in the sentence combined with your prior knowledge, and write what you think the underlined words mean on the lines provided.

1. And after a few days--then what? Would they let her go? Or would Billy <u>plead</u> for a few more?

   _____

2. But whatever he said, they would be <u>dreadfully</u> frightened and worried.

   _____

3. That would explain why the Public Health Service is in it. <u>Epidemic</u> control.

   _____

4. "Bulldoze my rosebush?" said Mrs. Fitzgibbon <u>indignantly</u>. "They will not!"

   _____

5. The door was stiff and it was heavy, and she could not get a good enough grip on either it or the cage wall to <u>exert</u> much pressure.

   _____

6. <u>Wearily</u>, she got up to climb the wall and try the door again.

   _____

7. But on the other side of the stone there was an <u>impasse</u>.

   _____

8. You couldn't help it if they put you in a <u>defective</u> cage.

   _____

9. "Now," he said, "we <u>shinny</u> down the stand like a fireman's pole."

   _____

Mrs. Frisby And The Rats Of NIMH Vocabulary Worksheet Assignment 10 Continued

Part II: Determining the Meaning -- Match the vocabulary words to their dictionary definitions.

____ 1. PLEAD   A. Make an earnest request

____ 2. DREADFULLY   B. Prevalent and spreading rapidly among many individuals

____ 3. EPIDEMIC   C. Imperfect; faulty

____ 4. INDIGNANTLY   D. Climb by using both hands and legs for gripping

____ 5. EXERT   E. Put forth or use energetically

____ 6. WEARILY   F. Terribly

____ 7. IMPASSE   G. In a tired or worn-out manner

____ 8. DEFECTIVE   H. In a manner expressing great anger or scorn

____ 9. SHINNY   I. A situation offering no escape

VOCABULARY ASSIGNMENT 11 *Mrs. Frisby And The Rats Of NIMH*

Part I: Using Prior Knowledge and Contextual Clues

Below are the sentences in which the vocabulary words appear in the text. Read the sentence. Use any clues you can find in the sentence combined with your prior knowledge, and write what you think the underlined words mean on the lines provided.

1. That morning there were two rats on <u>sentry</u> duty--one just inside the entrance to the rosebush, watching Mr. Fitzgibbon's house, another at the arch where Brutus had stood.

   _____

2. There was a table on it, covered with papers and one <u>vacant</u> space, where a chair had been placed for Mrs. Frisby.

   _____

3. Isabella, in ears, had run forward. "I want to stay, please," she had pleaded, looking <u>despairingly</u> at Justin.

   _____

4. "We'll give them another rear exit to block," Arthur had said <u>cryptically</u>. "One that's easier to find."

   _____

5. On this branch, up close to the trunk, she had a <u>vantage</u> point from which, herself unseen, she could look down on the rosebush and also see into the woods to a blackberry bramble.

   _____

6. Billy, after some argument, was <u>dispatched</u> to the back porch, where Mrs. Fitzgibbon was also watching.

   _____

7. The bush fought back, then yielded angrily, snapping and crackling before the <u>inexorable</u> thrust of steel.

   _____

8. A single sweep, and a third of it lay, a <u>writhing</u> heap of thorns, in a pile twenty feet away.

   _____

Mrs. Frisby And The Rats Of NIMH Vocabulary Worksheet Assignment 11 Continued

Part II: Determining the Meaning -- Match the vocabulary words to their dictionary definitions.

____ 1.   SENTRY   A. In a manner feeling or showing hopelessness

____ 2.   VACANT   B. Guard; watch

____ 3.   DESPAIRINGLY   C. Empty

____ 4.   CRYPTICALLY   D. Such that cannot be moved or influenced by persuasion

____ 5.   VANTAGE   E. Position that provides a clear, broad view

____ 6.   DISPATCHED   F. Making twisting or turning movements

____ 7.   INEXORABLE   G. Sent off on a specific errand

____ 8.   WRITHING   H. In a manner that is mysterious or obscure in meaning

VOCABULARY ANSWER KEY - *Mrs. Frisby And The Rats Of NIMH*

	1	2	3	4	5	6	7	8	9	10	11
1	B	I	B	C	F	E	F	E	G	A	B
2	D	F	A	I	B	A	H	I	E	F	C
3	E	J	H	G	J	C	E	G	J	B	A
4	H	E	I	E	H	J	D	H	B	H	H
5	I	D	C	J	D	G	A	C	I	E	E
6	J	A	D	D	C	H	J	D	F	G	G
7	F	B	J	A	I	B	B	B	A	I	D
8	A	G	G	B	G	D	C	J	D	C	F
9	G	H	E	H	A	I	G	A	C	D	
10	C	C	F	F	E	F	I	F	H		

DAILY LESSONS

LESSON ONE

Objectives
1. To introduce *Mrs. Frisby and the Rats of NIMH* unit
2. To discuss the pros and cons of using animals in laboratory tests
3. To write a paragraph expressing personal feelings regarding animal testing
4. To distribute books, study guides and other related materials
5. To introduce the Community Projects

Activity 1
Explain to students that they will be reading a book about rats who have been the subject of experiments in which they were injected with special serums that made them more advanced than other rats. In this activity, you will conduct a discussion about the pros and cons of using animals (such as mice, rats, and monkeys) in laboratory experiments. First, ask students to brainstorm why laboratories use animals in the first place. Then, create a T-chart on the board or on an overhead. Label the left-hand column pros and label the right-hand column cons. Give students sixty seconds to come up with at least one idea for each column. Then, as a class, fill in the T-chart on the board or overhead. You may want to have a student in the class keep a record of the T-chart to display on the bulletin board.

Some additional questions to ask may include: What is the benefit of using animals? Why do we test animals and not humans? What is the difference between a human and an animal? Why does society consider rodents as inferior to other animals like dogs, cats, and monkeys? Is it fair to perform tests on animals for the sake of human progress?

At the end of the activity, have students write a paragraph discussing their personal feelings on the topic. You may want to choose the best paragraphs to post on the bulletin board or select a few students to read their paragraphs to the class.

Activity 2
Distribute the materials students will use in this unit. Explain in detail how students are to use these materials.

Study Guides
Students should read the study guide questions for each reading assignment prior to beginning the reading assignment to get a feeling for what events and ideas are important in the section they are about to read. After reading the section, students will (as a class or individually) answer the questions to review the important events and ideas from that section of the book. Students should keep the study guides as study materials for the unit test.

Vocabulary
Prior to reading a reading assignment, students will do vocabulary work related to the section of the book they are about to read. Following the completion of the reading of the book, there will be a vocabulary review of all the words used in the vocabulary assignments. Students should keep their vocabulary work as study materials for the unit test.

Reading Assignment Sheet
You need to fill in the reading assignment sheet to let students know by when their reading has to be completed. You can either write the assignment sheet up on a side blackboard or bulletin board and leave it there for students to see each day, or you can make copies for each student to have. In either case, you should advise students to become very familiar with the reading assignments so they know what is expected of them.

Extra Activities Center

The Unit Resource Materials portion of this LitPlan contains suggestions for an extra library of related books and articles in your classroom as well as crossword and word search puzzles. Make an extra activities center in your room where you will keep these materials for students to use. (Bring the books and articles in from the library and keep several copies of the puzzles on hand.) Explain to students that these materials are available for students to use when they finish reading assignments or other class work early.

Non-fiction Assignment Sheet

Explain to students that they each are to read at least one non-fiction piece from the in-class library at some time during the unit. Students will fill out a non-fiction assignment sheet after completing the reading to help you (the teacher) evaluate their reading experiences and to help the students think about and evaluate their own reading experiences.

Books

Each school has its own rules and regulations regarding student use of school books. Advise students of the procedures that are normal for your school. Preview the book. Look at the covers, front matter, and index. Glance through at some of the drawings.

Activity 3

Introduce the Community Project by distributing the Project Sheet. Discuss the directions in detail.

COMMUNITY PROJECT

The Project

The Community Project is a small group project for use in conjunction with the novel *Mrs. Frisby and the Rats of NIMH*. Like the rats in the novel, students will be creating a Plan for their new community.

Objectives

1. Students will work cooperatively in a small group.

2. Students will develop research skills by using reference books, on-line databases, and other information sources.

3. Students will combine ideas and information from several sources.

4. Students will write a description and explanation of The Plan for their new community.

5. Students will organize ideas and information to emphasize key points for the audience.

Forming Work Groups

Either assign students to groups of 4 to 6 or allow them to choose their own group members. Then have the group choose a coordinator and recorder. Other tasks can be discussed on an as-needed basis.

NON-FICTION ASSIGNMENT SHEET
(To be completed after reading the required nonfiction article)

Name _____ Date _____

Title of Nonfiction Read _____

Written By _____ Publication Date _____

I. Factual Summary: Write a short summary of the piece you read.

II. Vocabulary
    1. With which vocabulary words in the piece did you encounter some degree of difficulty?

    2. How did you resolve your lack of understanding with these words?

III. Interpretation: What was the main point the author wanted you to get from reading his work?

IV. Criticism
    1. With which points of the piece did you agree or find easy to accept? Why?

    2. With which points of the piece did you disagree or find difficult to believe? Why?

V. Personal Response: What do you think about this piece? OR How does this piece influence your ideas?

COMMUNITY PROJECT SHEET

PROMPT
Mrs. Frisby and the Rats of NIMH tells the story of a very intelligent group of rats. The rats have become extremely advanced to the extent that they have created a community in which they can live completely independently of other animals and humans. This is their ideal community. What is your ideal community?

GETTING STARTED
Decide what kind of community you would like to create. What would make it perfect? Who would it be perfect for? You must include the following in your report:

1. Community's name (and explanation of the name)
2. Size of the community (and why)
3. Roles and responsibilities of the community members
4. Education
5. Government type and structure (democracy, monarchy, communism, etc.)
6. Location and physical description (including flora, fauna, weather conditions, natural resources, etc.)
7. Laws and punishments
8. Food (What kind of crops will you grow? Will you eat animals or will it be a vegetarian society? How will people acquire food? Will there be grocery stores?)
9. Religion
10. Available community resources (parks, YMCA, etc.)
11. Currency (Will there be a need for currency? If so, what will you use? If not, why?)

REQUIREMENTS
Prepare a written report describing the community. Be sure to include the eleven items discussed above. Make a poster outlining the key facts about the community. Be sure to include pictures or diagrams. You may want to include a map of your ideal community or create a diorama.

Be prepared to give a 5 - 10 minute oral report to the class. Each person in the group must participate. To make the presentation more authentic, you may want to dress and practice speaking the way the members of your community would.

LESSON TWO

Objectives
1. To preview the vocabulary and study questions for Assignment #1
2. To read Assignment #1
3. To give students practice reading orally
4. To evaluate students' oral reading

Activity 1
Show students how to preview the study questions and how to do the pre-reading vocabulary worksheet and then give them time to complete the worksheet.

Activity 2
Have students read Assignment #1 of *Mrs. Frisby and the Rats of NIMH* out loud in class. You probably know the best way to get readers with your class; pick students at random, ask for volunteers, or use whatever method works best for your group. If you have not yet completed an oral reading evaluation for your students this marking period, this would be a good opportunity to do so. A form is included with this unit for your convenience.

If students do not finish reading and answering the study guide questions for Assignment #1 in class, they should do so prior to your next class meeting.

ORAL READING EVALUATION *Mrs. Frisby and the Rats of NIMH*

Name _____ Class____ Date _____

SKILL	EXCELLENT	GOOD	AVERAGE	FAIR	POOR
Fluency	5	4	3	2	1
Clarity	5	4	3	2	1
Audibility	5	4	3	2	1
Pronunciation	5	4	3	2	1
_____	5	4	3	2	1
_____	5	4	3	2	1

Total _____   Grade _____

Comments:

LESSON THREE

Objectives
1. To review the main events and ideas from Assignment #1
2. To preview the study questions for Assignment #2
3. To familiarize students with the vocabulary for Assignment #2
4. To read Assignment #2
5. To give students practice reading orally
6. To evaluate students' oral reading

Activity 1
Give students a few minutes to formulate answers for the study guide questions for Assignment #1 and then discuss the answers to the questions in detail. Write the answers on the board or overhead transparency so students can have the correct answers for study purposes.

NOTE: It is a good practice in public speaking and leadership skills for individual students to take charge of leading the discussions of the study questions. Perhaps a different student could go to the front of the class and lead the discussion each day that the study questions are discussed in this unit. Of course, you should guide the discussion when appropriate and try to fill in any gaps students may leave. The study questions could really be handled in a number of different ways, including in small groups with group reports following. Occasionally you may want to use the multiple choice questions as quizzes to check students' reading comprehension. As a short review now and then, students could pair up for the first (or last, if you have time left at the end of a class period) few minutes of class to quiz each other from thes tudy questions. Mix up methods of reviewing the materials and checking comprehension throughout the unit so students don't get bored just answering the questions the same way each day. Variety in methods will also help address the different learning styles of your students.

Activity 2
Explain to students that there are many different kinds of conflicts: Character vs. Character, Character vs. Self, Character vs. Nature, and Character vs. Society. Discuss the meaning of each kind of conflict. Have students brainstorm examples of each kind of conflict. Students should think not only about other stories they may have read in school, but also television shows and movies they may have seen. For example, they may think of Harry Potter vs. Lord Voldemort as a type of Character vs. Character conflict.

Then, have students fill in the Conflict Type Chart for Assignment #1 of *Mrs. Frisby and the Rats of NIMH*. Review what students have come up with. An example of Character vs. Nature might be Timothy's illness. Or perhaps the students may have identified Mrs. Frisby vs. Dragon as a Character vs. Character conflict. Encourage students to hold onto their charts and fill in the conflicts they come across throughout the book.

Activity 3
Give students about fifteen minutes to preview the study questions for Assignment #2 of *Mrs. Frisby and the Rats of NIMH* and do the related vocabulary work.

Activity 4
Continue the oral reading evaluations while choosing students to read Assignment #2 orally in class. If students do not complete the reading assignment or the study guide questions in class, they should complete it prior to your next class meetings.

Conflict Type Chart

Character vs. Character	Character vs. Self	Character vs. Nature	Character vs. Society

LESSON FOUR

<u>Objectives</u>
1. To review the main events and ideas from Assignment #2
2. To preview the study questions for Assignment #3
3. To familiarize students with the vocabulary for Assignment #3
4. To read Assignment #3
5. To assign the nonfiction reading assignment and give students the opportunity to acquire materials for it

<u>Activity 1</u>
Quiz - Distribute quizzes for Assignment #2 and give students about 10 minutes to complete them. (Note: The quizzes may either be the short answer study guides or the multiple choice version.) Have students exchange papers. Grade the quizzes as a class. Collect the papers for recording the grades. (If you used the multiple choice version as a quiz, take a few minutes to discuss the answers for the short answer version if your students are using the short answer version for their study guides.)

<u>Activity 2</u>
Take students to the library/media center to find articles, books, etc. about non-fiction topics related to *Mrs. Frisby and the Rats of NIMH*. Suggested topics: gardening, farming/agricultural, utopic communities, animal rights, testing done on animals, pneumonia, Ground Hog Day, rats, mice, shrews, crows, owls, relationship between cats and rats, Ponce de Leon and the Fountain of Youth (the quest to live forever), and simple machines.

<u>Activity 3</u>
Tell students that prior to your next class meeting they need to have completed the pre-reading and reading work for Assignment #3.

LESSON FIVE

Objectives
1. To review the main events and ideas from Assignment #3
2. To preview the study questions for Assignment #4
3. To familiarize students with the vocabulary for Assignment #4
4. To read Assignment #4
5. To analyze characters presented so far in *Mrs. Frisby and the Rats of NIMH*
6. To practice working with spacial relationships

Activity 1
Give students a few minutes to formulate answers for the study guide questions for Assignment #3 and then discuss the answers to the questions in detail. Write the answers on the board or overhead transparency so students can have the correct answers for study purposes. You may want to discuss new conflicts the students have identified and recorded in the Conflict Type Chart.

Activity 2
Give students about fifteen minutes to preview the study questions for Assignment #4 of *Mrs. Frisby and the Rats of NIMH* and do the related vocabulary work.

Activity 3
On the board, have students brainstorm all of the characters presented thus far in *Mrs. Frisby and the Rats of NIMH*. Don't forget characters like the shrew, Dragon, and Mr. Fitzgibbon. Now, have each student draw a geometric shape (square, circle, triangle, etc.) for each character on his/her own paper. Students should keep in mind size and how the sizes change from character to character. Now have the students write a one or two sentence explanation of the shape and how it "fits" the character. Call on students to come to the board and draw their shape for one character. Then have the students discuss the shape they drew and why.

Extension to Activity #3: Have students color their shapes and paste them onto a piece of construction paper. Encourage students to paste their shapes thoughtfully (Which characters are connected? Which characters are close? What are the relationships between the characters?). Then, have student write a description of their collage. Post the best collages on the bulletin board.

LESSON SIX

Objectives
1. To review the main events and ideas from Assignment #4
2. To preview the study questions for Assignment #5
3. To familiarize students with the vocabulary for Assignment #5
4. To read Assignment #5
5. To give students practice reading orally

Activity 1
Quiz - Distribute quizzes for Assignment #4 and give students about 10 minutes to complete them. (Note: The quizzes may either be the short answer study guides or the multiple choice version.) Have students exchange papers. Grade the quizzes as a class. Collect the papers for recording the grades. (If you used the multiple choice version as a quiz, take a few minutes to discuss the answers for the short answer version if your students are using the short answer version for their study guides.)

While students have their study guides out, preview the study questions for Assignment #5.

Activity 2
Do the vocabulary worksheet for Assignment #5 orally in class together.

Activity 3
Have students read Assignment #5 of *Mrs. Frisby and the Rats of NIMH* out loud in class. You probably know the best way to get readers with your class; pick students at random, ask for volunteers, or use whatever method works best for your group. If you have not yet completed an oral reading evaluation for your students this marking period, this would be a good opportunity to do so. A form is included with this unit for your convenience.

If students do not finish reading and answering the study guide questions for Assignment #5 in class, they should do so prior to your next class meeting.

LESSON SEVEN

<u>Objectives</u>
1. To review the main events and ideas from Assignment #5
2. To preview the study questions for Assignment #6
3. To familiarize students with the vocabulary for Assignment #6
4. To read Assignment #6
5. To distribute Writing Assignment #1
6. To practice writing to inform
7. To evaluate students' writing skills
8. To exercise students' basic analytical skills by comparing and contrasting

Activity 1
Give students a few minutes to formulate answers for the study guide questions for Assignment #5 and then discuss the answers to the questions in detail. Write the answers on the board or overhead transparency so students can have the correct answers for study purposes.

Activity 2
Give students about fifteen minutes to preview the study questions for Assignment #6 of *Mrs. Frisby and the Rats of NIMH* and do the related vocabulary work. Instruct students to complete the assignment for the next meeting if they have not finished it in the allotted time.

Activity 3
Distribute Writing Assignment #1 and discuss the directions in detail. Give students the remainder of the period to work on the assignment. Assign a due date and decide on a length for the composition.

WRITING ASSIGNMENT #1 - *Mrs. Frisby and the Rats of NIMH*
Writing to Inform

PROMPT

Most of the main characters in *Mrs. Frisby and the Rats of NIMH* are animals. These animals have many human qualities like the ability to talk, think, and read. Your job is to write a composition in which you compare and contrast one character from the story and his/her real-life equivalent.

PREWRITING

Choose one of the following character/animal combinations: Mrs. Frisby/mouse, Mr. Ages/mouse, Nicodemus/rat, Justin/rat, Dragon/cat, The Owl/owl, Jeremy/crow. Using the internet, encyclopedia, and other resources, research the animal you have chosen. Make sure to take careful notes. Your notes should include topics like: appearance, habitat, food source, and other interesting facts. Then, reread through the parts in the book where your character appears and take notes on similar topics as described by the author.

DRAFTING

Introduce your character/animal combination in the first paragraph. Tell why you chose this particular pair to write about. Give a preview of what the rest of the paper will be about. Then write several paragraphs about your character and animal choice. Each paragraph should have a main idea and supporting details. Since this is a compare and contrast essay, you may want to compare and contrast one topic about your character/animal combination in each paragraph. For example, your first paragraph might be a comparison and contrast of the appearance of Mrs. Frisby vs. real life mice. Then your second paragraph might be about the habitat of Mrs. Frisby vs. real life mice. Your last paragraph should summarize the information in the report.

PEER EDITING/PROOFREADING

When you finish the rough draft of your paper, ask a student who sits near you to read it. After reading your rough draft, he/she should tell you what he/she liked best about your work, which parts were difficult to understand, and ways in which your work could be improved. Reread your paper considering your critic's comments, and make the corrections you think are necessary. Ask your classmate what he/she thought of the character/animal you chose for your assignment.

Do a final proofreading of your paper double-checking your grammar, spelling, organization, and the clarity of your ideas.

FINAL DRAFT

Follow your teacher's directions for making a final copy of your report.

WRITING EVALUATION FORM - *Mrs. Frisby and the Rats of NIMH*

Name _____ Date _____

Grade _____

Circle One For Each Item:

Grammar:	correct errors noted on paper
Spelling:	correct errors noted on paper
Punctuation:	correct errors noted on paper
Legibility:	excellent good fair poor
_____	excellent good fair poor
_____	excellent good fair poor

Strengths:

Weaknesses:

Comments/Suggestions:

LESSON EIGHT

<u>Objectives</u>
1. To review the main events and ideas from Assignment #6
2. To preview the study questions for Assignment #7
3. To familiarize students with the vocabulary for Assignment #7
4. To read Assignment #7
5. To give students practice reading orally

<u>Activity 1</u>
Give students a few minutes to formulate answers for the study guide questions for Assignment #6 and then discuss the answers to the questions in detail. Write the answers on the board or overhead transparency so students can have the correct answers for study purposes.

<u>Activity 2</u>
Give students about fifteen minutes to preview the study questions for Assignment #7 of *Mrs. Frisby and the Rats of NIMH* and do the related vocabulary work.

<u>Activity 3</u>
Read Assignment #7 aloud or silently. Instruct students to complete the vocabulary and reading for Assignment #7 as homework if they do not finish by the end of the class time.

LESSON NINE

Objectives
1. To review the main events and ideas from Assignment #7
2. To preview the study questions for Assignment #8
3. To familiarize students with the vocabulary for Assingment #8
4. To read Assignment #8
5. To participate in writing conferences
6. To revise Writing Assignment #1 based on the teacher's suggestions

Activity 1
Give students a few minutes to formulate answers for the study guide questions for Assignment #7 and then discuss the answers to the questions in detail. Write the answers on the board or overhead transparency so students can have the correct answers for study purposes.

Activity 2
Give students about fifteen minutes to preview the study questions for Assignment #8 of *Mrs. Frisby and the Rats of NIMH* and do the related vocabulary work.

Activity 3
Have students read Assignment #8 and complete the study guide activities silently while you conduct writing conferences with each student for Writing Assignment #1. Make sure to tell students when to turn in their revised Assignment #1s.

LESSON TEN

Objectives
1. To review the main events and ideas from Assignment #8
2. To preview the study questions for Assignment #9
3. To familiarize students with the vocabulary for Assignment #9
4. To read Assignment #9
5. To distribute Writing Assignment #2
6. To practice creative writing
7. To practice thinking logically by filling in events from a past point to a present point in time
8. To further explore the character of Nicodemus

Activity 1
Give students a few minutes to formulate answers for the study guide questions for Assignment #8 and then discuss the answers to the questions in detail. Write the answers on the board or overhead transparency so students can have the correct answers for study purposes.

Activity 2
Give students about fifteen minutes to preview the study questions for Assignment #9 of *Mrs. Frisby and the Rats of NIMH* and do the related vocabulary work. Tell students they should complete this vocabulary assignment and read Assignment #9 prior to your next class meeting.

Activity 3
Distribute Writing Assignment #2 and discuss the directions in detail. Give students the remainder of the period to work on the assignment. Assign a due date and decide on a length for the composition.

WRITING ASSIGNMENT #2 - *Mrs. Frisby and the Rats of NIMH*
Creative Writing

PROMPT
In the chapter entitled "The Boniface Estate," Nicodemus explains to Mrs. Frisby that he wishes to write a book about the journey the rats experienced after their escape from the lab and before they settled on the farm. He tells her that some parts of the journey were pleasant while others were terrible (like how he lost his eye). Nicodemus has made notes about all of it. What do you think are some of the adventures the rats encountered that Nicodemus has not yet told Mrs. Frisby?

PREWRITING
Write the memoirs of Nicodemus using details from the story. You might want to explain how Nicodemus lost his eye or what happened between the time the rats left the Boniface Estate and settled on the farm. Brainstorm a list of several adventures they could have encountered and organize them in chronological order.

DRAFTING
You are writing Nicodemus's memoirs so you are to write in the first person.

There are several ways you could write these memoirs. You could write them like journal entries. Or you could write your memoir like a story with a beginning, middle, and end. In either case, your composition should progress in chronological order. This kind of composition is different from an informative or persuasive essay because it does not follow the intro/body/conclusion format. Be creative! Have fun with your story!

PEER EDITING/PROOFREADING
When you finish the rough draft of your story, ask a student who sits near you to read it. After reading your rough draft, he/she should tell you what he/she liked best about your work, which parts were difficult to understand, and ways in which your work could be improved. Reread your work considering your critic's comments, and make the corrections you think are necessary. Ask your classmate what he/she thought of each of the characters/events you chose for your assignment. Do a final proofreading of your paper double-checking your grammar, spelling, organization, and the clarity of your ideas.

FINAL DRAFT
Follow your teacher's directions for making a final copy of your report.

LESSON ELEVEN

<u>Objectives</u>
1. To review the main events and ideas from Assignment #9
2. To preview the study questions for Assignment #10
3. To familiarize students with the vocabulary for Assignment #10
4. To read Assignment #10

<u>Activity 1</u>
Give students a few minutes to formulate answers for the study guide questions for Assignment #9 and then discuss the answers to the questions in detail. Write the answers on the board or overhead transparency so students can have the correct answers for study purposes.

<u>Activity 2</u>
Give students about fifteen minutes to preview the study questions for Assignment #10 of *Mrs. Frisby and the Rats of NIMH* and do the related vocabulary work.

<u>Activity 3</u>
Read Assignment #10 aloud or silently. Tell students the vocabulary and reading work for Assignment #10 should be completed prior to your next class meeting.

LESSON TWELVE

Objectives
1. To review the main events and ideas from Assignment #10
2. To preview the study questions for Assignment #11
3. To familiarize students with the vocabulary for Assignment #11
4. To read Assignment #11
5. To individually discuss and evaluate students' writing skills
6. To revise Writing Assignment #2 based on teacher's suggestions

Activity 1
Give students a few minutes to formulate answers for the study guide questions for Assignment #10 and then discuss the answers to the questions in detail. Write the answers on the board or overhead transparency so students can have the correct answers for study purposes.

Activity 2
Preview the study questions for Assignment #11 of *Mrs. Frisby and the Rats of NIMH* and do the related vocabulary work orally together in class.

Activity 3
Have students read Assignment #11 silently while you conduct writing conferences with each student for Writing Assignment #2. Make sure to tell students when to turn in their revised Writing Assignment #2s.

LESSON THIRTEEN

<u>Objectives</u>
1. To review the main events and ideas from Assignment #11
2. To distribute Writing Assignment #3
3. To practice writing to persuade
4. To further consider the different points of view of Nicodemus and Jenner

<u>Activity 1</u>
Quiz - Distribute quizzes for Assignment #11 and give students about 10 minutes to complete them. (Note: The quizzes may either be the short answer study guides or the multiple choice version.) Have students exchange papers. Grade the quizzes as a class. Collect the papers for recording the grades. (If you used the multiple choice version as a quiz, take a few minutes to discuss the answers for the short answer version if your students are using the short answer version for their study guides.)

<u>Activity 2</u>
Distribute Writing Assignment #3. Discuss the directions in detail and give students ample time to complete the assignment. Give students the remainder of the class period to work on this assignment.

Determine the amount of time your students will need to complete this assignment to your standards and tell them when the paper will be due. Tell students exactly what you expect regarding length of the story and the elements on which they will be graded. This can be a simple composition of a page or two, simply to introduce the idea of an adventure story, or it can be as elaborate and demanding as you think your students can handle.

WRITING ASSIGNMENT #3 - *Mrs. Frisby and the Rats of NIMH*
Writing to Persuade

PROMPT
Nicodemus explains to Mrs. Frisby that the rats have created The Plan because most of the community members do not like stealing from others in order to live. However, there are rats in the community like Jenner and his friends who think that stealing is a perfectly acceptable way of living and don't want to give up the comfortable home they have made on Mr. Fitzgibbon's farm. Do you agree with Nicodemus or Jenner? Your assignment is to write a speech in which you persuade the community to side with either Nicodemus or Jenner.

PREWRITING
Choose a side: Nicodemus or Jenner? Then, make a list of positive outcomes for either leaving or not leaving the cave. Finally, brainstorm reasons your opponent's argument will not be beneficial to the community.

DRAFTING
Make an introductory statement in which you describe your position and the argument you support (Nicodemus or Jenner?). Ask your fellow community members to support your position/cause.

Use one paragraph for each of your reasons. Then write a closing statement in which you again ask the community members to side with you against your opponent.

REVISING
When you finish the rough draft, ask a student who sits near you to read it. After reading your rough draft, he/she should tell you what he/she liked best about your work, which parts were difficult to understand, and ways in which your work could be improved. Reread your paper considering your critic's comments, and make the corrections you think are necessary. Ask your classmate what he/she thought of each of the characters/events you chose for your assignment. Do a final proofreading of your paper double-checking your grammar, spelling, organization, and the clarity of your ideas.

FINAL DRAFT
Follow your teacher's guidelines for completing the final draft of your paper.

LESSON FOURTEEN

Objectives
To review all of the vocabulary work done in this unit

Activity
Choose one (or more) of the vocabulary review activities listed below and spend your class period as directed in the activity. Some of the materials for these review activities are located in the Vocabulary Resource Materials section in this LitPlan.

VOCABULARY REVIEW ACTIVITIES

1. Divide your class into two teams and have an old-fashioned spelling or definition bee.

2. Give each of your students (or students in groups of two, three or four) a *Mrs. Frisby and the Rats of NIMH* Vocabulary Word Search Puzzle. The person (group) to find all of the vocabulary words in the puzzle first wins.

3. Give students a *Mrs. Frisby and the Rats of NIMH* Vocabulary Word Search Puzzle without the word list. The person or group to find the most vocabulary words in the puzzle wins.

4. Use a *Mrs. Frisby and the Rats of NIMH* Vocabulary Crossword Puzzle. Put the puzzle onto a transparency on the overhead projector (so everyone can see it), and do the puzzle together as a class.

5. Give students a *Mrs. Frisby and the Rats of NIMH* Vocabulary Matching Worksheet to do.

6. Divide your class into two teams. Use *Mrs. Frisby and the Rats of NIMH* vocabulary words with their letters jumbled as a word list. Student 1 from Team A faces off against Student 1 from Team B. You write the first jumbled word on the board. The first student (1A or 1B) to unscramble the word wins the chance for his/her team to score points. If 1A wins the jumble, go to student 2A and give him/her a definition. He/she must give you the correct spelling of the vocabulary word which fits that definition. If he/she does, Team A scores a point, and you give student 3A a definition for which you expect a correctly spelled matching vocabulary word. Continue giving Team A definitions until some team member makes an incorrect response. An incorrect response sends the game back to the jumbled-word face off, this time with students 2A and 2B. Instead of repeating giving definitions to the first few students of each team, continue with the student after the one who gave the last incorrect response on the team. For example, if Team B wins the jumbled-word face-off, and student 5B gave the last incorrect answer for Team B, you would start this round of definition questions with student 6B, and so on. The team with the most points wins!

7. Have students write a story in which they correctly use as many vocabulary words as possible. Have students read their compositions orally! Post the most original compositions on your bulletin board!

LESSON FIFTEEN

<u>Objectives</u>
1. To review the Conflict Type Chart from the beginning of the unit
2. To discuss the ideas and themes from *Mrs. Frisby and the Rats of NIMH* in greater detail
3. To have students exercise their critical thinking skills
4. To try to relate some of the ideas in *Mrs. Frisby and the Rats of NIMH* to the students' lives

Activity 1
Review the Conflict Type Chart that students were completing while reading *Mrs. Frisby and the Rats of NIMH*. You may want to give students a few minutes to finish up any other conflicts they can think of. Then, discuss the types of conflicts the students found in the story.

Activity 2
Choose the questions from the Extra Discussion Questions/Writing Assignments which seem most appropriate for your students. A class discussion of these questions is most effective if students have been given the opportunity to formulate answers to the questions prior to the discussion. To this end, you may either have all the students formulate answers to all the questions, divide your class into groups and assign one or more questions to each group, or you could assign one question to each student in your class. The option you choose will make a difference in the amount of class time needed for this activity.

Activity 3
After students have had ample time to formulate answer to the questions, begin your class discussion of the questions and the ideas presented by the questions. Be sure students take notes during the discussion so they have information to study for the test.

NOTE: The use of graphic organizers may be helpful to students in preparing their answers. Encourage them to use any diagrams or graphics that they feel are necessary.

EXTRA WRITING ASSIGNMENTS/DISCUSSION QUESTIONS - *Mrs. Frisby and the Rats of NIMH*

Interpretation

1. From what point of view is the story told. Why is that important?
2. What is the setting and what does it add to the story?
3. Are the characters in *Mrs. Frisby and the Rats of NIMH* stereotypes/archtypes? If so, give specific examples and explain the usefulness of employing stereotypes/archtypes in the book. If they are not, explain how they merit individuality.
4. What are the main conflicts in the story, and how are they resolved?
5. What are three main themes presented in *Mrs. Frisby and the Rats of NIMH*?
6. If Mrs. Frisby had known about the Rats of NIMH before the death of her husband, would the story have been different? Why or why not?
7. If Justin had not discovered the Toy Tinker and his truck, how do you think the story of the rats would have been different?
8. How do you think Nicodemus would describe Jenner?
9. What do you think was the purpose of Dr. Schultz's tests and research? What do you think the results would have proven?

Critical

1. Explain the significance of the title *Mrs. Frisby and the Rats of NIMH*.
2. Compare and contrast Nicodemus and Jenner.
3. What is Dragon's purpose in the story?
4. What is Justin's purpose in the story?
5. What is Jeremy's purpose in the story?
6. What is the Owl's purpose in the story?
7. List the protagonists and the antagonists in the story and justify your answer. Are they clear cut? Did you find it difficult to come up with a list? Why or why not?
8. Who is the main character of *Mrs. Frisby and the Rats of NIMH*? Justify your answer.
9. Describe O'Brien's writing style. How does it influence our perception of the story?

10. How are the animal characters in the story different from humans? How are they the same?
11. Name several ways in which the ability to read improved the quality of life for the rats.
12. Why do you think the author added Isabella into the story?
13. Describe the relationship between the animals and Mr. Fitzgibbon.

Critical/Personal Response

1. Is the story of *Mrs. Frisby and the Rats of NIMH* believable? Why or why not?
2. Is *Mrs. Frisby and the Rats of NIMH* more than just an adventure story? Why or why not?
3. Choose another title for this book and justify your choice.
4. Which character in the book is the least honorable? Most honorable? Justify your answer.
5. While you were reading, did you want to warn or communicate with any of the characters in *Mrs. Frisby and the Rats of NIMH*? If so, which characters and when?
6. How do you think Mrs. Frisby was feeling when she entered the Owl's hollow? How would you have felt?
7. Would you like to live forever (or for an unusually long time) like the rats?
8. Why might someone want to live forever?
9. What are the benefits of reading? What are the negatives of not being able to read? Find examples in the book.

Personal Response

1. If you could trade places with one of the characters from the story, who would it be and why?
2. Would you recommend this book to a friend? Why or why not
3. Which character is your favorite? Why?

LESSON SIXTEEN

<u>Objectives</u>
1. To widen the breadth of students' knowledge about topics related to the novel
2. To check students' non-fiction reading assignments

<u>Activity</u>
Ask each student to give a brief oral report about the non-fiction articles he/she read for the unit project assignment. Your criteria for evaluating this report will vary depending on the level of your students. You may wish for students to give a complete report without using notes of any kind, or you may want students to read directly from a written report, or you may want to do something in between these two extremes. Just make students aware of your criteria in ample time for them to prepare their reports.

Start with one student's report. After that, ask if anyone else in the class has read on a topic related to the first student's report. If no one has, choose another student at random. After each report, be sure to ask if anyone has a report related to the one just completed. That will help keep a continuity during the discussion of the reports. After all reports on a topic are given, take a minute to hold a short class discussion about the information students have just heard.

LESSON SEVENTEEN

<u>Objectives</u>
1. To evaluate and discuss students' Community Project
2. To practice public speaking

<u>Activity</u>
Ask each group to give a 5 - 10 presentation about the community they created for their Community Project. Students should use the poster and/or diorama they created as a visual aid. Your criteria for evaluating this report will vary depending on the level of your students. You may wish for students to give a complete report without using notes of any kind, or you may want students to read directly from a written report, or you may want to do something in between these two extremes. Just make students aware of your criteria in ample time for them to prepare their reports.

After all projects have been presented, take a minute to hold a short class discussion about the reports students have just heard.

LESSON EIGHTEEN

<u>Objectives</u>
To review the main ideas and events in *Mrs. Frisby and the Rats of NIMH*

<u>Activity</u>
Choose one of the review games/activities suggested below and spend your class time as directed.

REVIEW GAMES/ACTIVITIES

1. Ask the class to make up a unit test for *Mrs. Frisby and the Rats of NIMH*. The test should have 4 sections: matching, true/false, short answer, and essay. Students may use 1/2 period to make the test and then swap papers and use the other 1/2 class period to take a test a classmate has devised. (open book) You may want to use the unit test included in this packet or take questions from the students' unit tests to formulate your own test.

2. Take 1/2 period for students to make up true and false questions (including the answers). Collect the papers and divide the class into two teams. Draw a big tic-tac-toe board on the chalk board. Make one team X and one team O. Ask questions to each side, giving each student one turn. If the question is answered correctly, that students' team's letter (X or O) is placed in the box. If the answer is incorrect, no letter is placed in the box. The object is to get three in a row like tic-tac-toe. You may want to keep track of the number of games won for each team.

3. Take 1/2 period for students to make up questions (true/false and short answer). Collect the questions. Divide the class into two teams. You'll alternate asking questions to individual members of teams A & B (like in a spelling bee). The question keeps going from A to B until it is correctly answered, then a new question is asked. A correct answer does not allow the team to get another question. Correct answers are +2 points; incorrect answers are -1 point.

4. Have students pair up and quiz each other from their study guides and class notes.

5. Give students an *Mrs. Frisby and the Rats of NIMH* crossword puzzle to complete.

6. Divide your class into two teams. Use the *Mrs. Frisby and the Rats of NIMH* unit word list. Student 1 from Team A faces off against Student 1 from Team B. You write the first jumbled word on the board. The first student (1A or 1B) to unscramble the word wins the chance for his/her team to score points. If 1A wins the jumble, go to student 2A and give him/her a clue. He/she must give you the correct word which matches that clue. If he/she does, Team A scores a point, and you give student 3A a clue for which you expect another correct response. Continue giving Team A clues until some team member makes an incorrect response. An incorrect response sends the game back to the jumbled-word face off, this time with students 2A and 2B. Instead of repeating giving clues to the first few students of each team, continue with the student after the one who gave the last incorrect response on the team. For example, if Team B wins the jumbled-word face-off, and student 5B gave the last incorrect answer for Team B, you would start this round of clue questions with student 6B, and so on. The team with the most points wins!

7. Play What's My Line?. This is similar to the old television show. Students assume the roles of different characters from the epic. One student gives clues to the class, or to a panel of contestants. The contestants try to guess the identity of the guest. Students may enjoy assisting you in creating rules and procedures for the game.

8. Play Jeopardy. Divide the class into two groups. Assign each group a category or book from the epic and have them devise answers for that category. Play the game according to the television show procedures.

9. Play Drawing in the Details. This is similar to Pictionary. Divide students into teams. A student from one team draws a scene from the epic. (You may want to specify the Book or section.) Drawings should be kept simple, to keep the pace lively. Students in the opposing team locate the scene in their books and read it aloud. If they are incorrect, the illustrator's team has a chance to guess. Involve students in setting up a scoring system and any other necessary rules.

LESSON NINETEEN

Objectives
To test the students understanding of the main ideas and themes in Mrs. Frisby and the Rats of NIMH

Activity
Distribute the unit tests, give students ample time to complete them, and collect the tests when students finish. Remember to collect assigned books prior to the end of the class period.

NOTE: There are 5 different unit tests included in this LitPlan Teacher Pack. Two are short answer, two are multiple choice. There is one advanced short answer test. Use the matching key for short answer unit test 2 to check the matching section of the advanced short answer unit test. The answers to the short answer test will be based on the discussions you have had during class and should be graded accordingly. You should choose the tests and/or test parts which best suit your needs. Matching and short answer tests have answer keys. For essay type questions, grade according to your own criteria based on class discussions and the level of your students. Also, you will need to choose vocabulary words to read orally for the vocabulary sections of the short answer tests.

UNIT TESTS

Mrs. Frisby And The Rats Of NIMH Short Answer Unit Test 1

I. Matching/Identify

____ 1. JEREMY   A. Cat that killed Jonathan Frisby

____ 2. AGES   B. Dr. Schultz's female assistant

____ 3. FITZGIBBON   C. Estate where the rats stayed after NIMH

____ 4. JENNER   D. He takes Mrs. Frisby to see the owl.

____ 5. DRAGON   E. He captures Mrs. Frisby under a colander.

____ 6. ISABELLA   F. She puts the sleeping powder in the cat's bowl.

____ 7. BRUTUS   G. Where Jenner and his group were stealing tools: ____'s Hardware

____ 8. JUSTIN   H. He makes powders and potions.

____ 9. HENDERSON   I. Nicodemus's best friend growing up

____ 10. BONIFACE   J. Doctor who runs NIMH

____ 11. SCHULTZ   K. Owner of the Boniface Estate

____ 12. BILLY   L. Huge rat revived after breathing the gas

____ 13. JULIE   M. Young female rat Mrs. Frisby encounters in the library

____ 14. GORDON   N. The farmer

____ 15. FRISBY   O. Helps Mrs. Frisby escape from Billy's cage

II. Short Answer

1. Why does Mrs. Frisby worry about the trip to see Mr. Ages and why does she eventually go?

2. Why must all the animals move out of the garden when winter is over?

3. Why didn't the Frisbys make their winter home in the barn lofts or attics like some other field mice?

4. What is the owl's advice to Mrs. Frisby?

5. What does Mrs. Frisby learn from Isabella about life in the rat colony?

6. How does Dr. Schultz organize the rats?

7. According to Nicodemus, what is the reason for their captivity?

8. How did the rats keep themselves from being detected by the caretaker-gardener?

9. What did the rats do late into the night all winter long while staying at the Boniface Estate?

10. Why are rats the most hated animals on earth, according to Nicodemus?

11. Describe what Nicodemus and the rats found in the Toy Tinker's truck.

12. What is a "rat race"?

13. Why do the rats want to destroy the machinery and the other conveniences of their current home?

14. What did the rats do to make the exterminators believe it was an ordinary rat hole?

15. Why does Mrs. Frisby decide to tell the children about NIMH?

III. Composition
1. What are three main themes presented in *Mrs. Frisby and the Rats of NIMH*? Briefly describe each in a sentence or two.

2. Choose three of the following characters and fully explain the purpose of each in the story: Dragon, Justin, Jeremy, the owl, Jonathan Frisby.

3. How are the animal characters in the story different from humans? How are they the same?

IV. Vocabulary

Write the vocabulary words you are given. After writing them down, go back and write in their definitions.

Word	Definition
1	
2	
3	
4	
5	
6	
7	
8	
9	
10	

Mrs. Frisby And The Rats Of NIMH Short Answer Unit Test 1 Answer Key

I. Matching/Identify

D	1.	JEREMY	A.	Cat that killed Jonathan Frisby
H	2.	AGES	B.	Dr. Schultz's female assistant
N	3.	FITZGIBBON	C.	Estate where the rats stayed after NIMH
I	4.	JENNER	D.	He takes Mrs. Frisby to see the owl.
A	5.	DRAGON	E.	He captures Mrs. Frisby under a colander.
M	6.	ISABELLA	F.	She puts the sleeping powder in the cat's bowl.
L	7.	BRUTUS	G.	Where Jenner and his group were stealing tools: ____'s Hardware
O	8.	JUSTIN	H.	He makes powders and potions.
G	9.	HENDERSON	I.	Nicodemus's best friend growing up
C	10.	BONIFACE	J.	Doctor who runs NIMH
J	11.	SCHULTZ	K.	Owner of the Boniface Estate
E	12.	BILLY	L.	Huge rat revived after breathing the gas
B	13.	JULIE	M.	Young female rat Mrs. Frisby encounters in the library
K	14.	GORDON	N.	The farmer
F	15.	FRISBY	O.	Helps Mrs. Frisby escape from Billy's cage

II. Short Answer

1. Why does Mrs. Frisby worry about the trip to see Mr. Ages and why does she eventually go?
   The trip is a long, hard journey that is risky unless she is extremely cautious. She cannot take the shortest route because it would lead her too close to the farmhouse and the barn, where the cat stalks relentlessly. Ordinarily, she does not set out so late in the day, for fear that darkness will come too soon. She decides to leave because Timothy is so sick she obviously cannot wait until the next day.

2. Why must all the animals move out of the garden when winter is over?
   As soon as the weather allows, Farmer Fitzgibbon's tractor comes rumbling through, pulling the sharp-bladed plow through the soil, turning over every foot of it. No animal caught in the garden that day is likely to escape alive.

3. Why didn't the Frisbys make their winter home in the barn lofts or attics like some other field mice?
   The Frisbys always go to the garden, preferring the relative safety and freedom of the outdoors.

4. What is the owl's advice to Mrs. Frisby?
   He tells her to go see the rats. She should tell Justin, the sentry guarding the door, who she is--and she should ask to see a rat named Nicodemus. The owl recommends doing whatever the rats ask of her.

5. What does Mrs. Frisby learn from Isabella about life in the rat colony?
   She learns that they have a grain room (presumable for food storage); the females sometimes go to meetings and sometimes not; Nicodemus seems to be the leader; they have a Plan for the future that some rats do not like; and one, named Jenner, has deserted.

6. How does Dr. Schultz organize the rats?
   He splits them up into groups A, B, and C. There are twenty in group A, twenty in group B, and 23 in group C. The cages and collars for the rats are numbered accordingly. The rats in the A group will receive injections of series A and training. The rats in B will receive injections of series B and training. Group C will be the control group and only receive a prick from a plain needle.

7. According to Nicodemus, what is the reason for their captivity?
   Dr. Schultz is a neurologist--that is, an expert on brains, nerves, intelligence, and how people learn things. By experimenting on the rats, he hopes to find out whether certain injections can help them learn more and faster.

8. How did the rats keep themselves from being detected by the caretaker-gardener?
   They had to haul all their empty tin cans and other trash far from the house. They cleaned up after themselves carefully. They learned to use the water taps and the dusting cloths they found in the kitchen closet.

9. What did the rats do late into the night all winter long while staying at the Boniface Estate?
   They studied the books in the library and taught themselves to write.

10. Why are rats the most hated animals on earth, according to Nicodemus?
    They are the most hated animals because they steal food.

11. Describe what Nicodemus and the rats found in the Toy Tinker's truck.
    The rats found the Toy Tinker's tools. The tools were small enough for the rats to use.

12. What is a "rat race"?
    A "rat race" is a race where, no matter how fast you run, you don't get anywhere.

13. Why do the rats want to destroy the machinery and the other conveniences of their current home?
    The rats want to destroy the machinery because if the cave is later discovered, it would only look like debris, and their secret wouldn't be discovered. Also, they know their first few years in Thorn Valley are going to be difficult, and they want to remove the temptation to come back to their comfortable home.

14. What did the rats do to make the exterminators believe it was an ordinary rat hole?
    They moved all of their equipment to the cave and sealed it off. They ripped up all the carpet and wiring. They brought garbage into the storeroom. They destroyed the elegant archway. They dug a false back door.

15. Why does Mrs. Frisby decide to tell the children about NIMH?
    She believes her children have a right to know about their father and the possibility that they might be different from other mice because of their father's injections.

IV. Vocabulary

Write the vocabulary words you are given. After writing them down, go back and write in their definitions.

Word	Definition
1	
2	
3	
4	
5	
6	
7	
8	
9	
10	

Mrs. Frisby And The Rats Of NIMH Short Answer Unit Test 2

I. Matching

____ 1. PNEUMONIA   A. Timothy's illness

____ 2. BUSH   B. Paul thinks the Public Health Service is investigating this disease in rats.

____ 3. SHREW   C. Rats get this through the maze floor when they go the wrong way.

____ 4. ELECTROCUTED   D. Billy uses it as a rat trap.

____ 5. TWENTY   E. Mrs. Frisby's neighbor

____ 6. MOVING   F. ____ RATS INVADE HARDWARE STORE

____ 7. LIBRARY   G. The men said they could capture the rats because they had become ___.

____ 8. THREE   H. Number of rats that escaped from NIMH

____ 9. READING   I. Where Mrs. Frisby waits for her first meeting with Nicodemus

____ 10. MOUNTAINS   J. Thorny covering over the entrance to the rat hole: rose ____

____ 11. TOOLS   K. They tell Nicodemus to go to the owl.

____ 12. CHIPMUNKS   L. The real treasure the rats find in the Toy Tinker's truck

____ 13. COLANDER   M. Jenner and his group were ___ when trying to steal a motor.

____ 14. RABIES   N. Number of rat groups in the NIMH lab

____ 15. OWL   O. The Plan is to learn to live without ___.

____ 16. CARELESS   P. Mrs. Frisby worries about this while Timothy is sick: ___ Day

____ 17. SHOCK   Q. National Forest where the rats decide to move while at Boniface: Thorn ___

____ 18. WRITE   R. The oldest animal in the woods who gives advice

____ 19. STEALING   S. Most important skill the rats learn in NIMH

____ 20. MECHANIZED   T. The rats spent their time reading and learning to ___ at Boniface Estate.

II. Identify

____ 1. JONATHAN   A. Cat that killed Jonathan Frisby

____ 2. JEREMY   B. Huge rat revived after breathing the gas

____ 3. AGES   C. Male assistant in the NIMH lab

____ 4. FITZGIBBON   D. He makes powders and potions.

____ 5. JENNER   E. Doctor who runs NIMH

____ 6. DRAGON   F. Helps Mrs. Frisby escape from Billy's cage

____ 7. ISABELLA   G. He captures Mrs. Frisby under a colander.

____ 8. BRUTUS   H. Yellow canary, once the Fitzgibbons' pet

____ 9. JUSTIN   I. Mrs. Frisby's husband

____ 10. SCHULTZ   J. He takes Mrs. Frisby to see the owl.

____ 11. GEORGE   K. The farmer

____ 12. BILLY   L. Young female rat Mrs. Frisby encounters in the library

____ 13. JULIE   M. Dr. Schultz's female assistant

____ 14. FRISBY   N. She puts the sleeping powder in the cat's bowl.

____ 15. PORGY   O. Nicodemus's best friend growing up

III. Short Answer

1. What was the purpose of Mrs. Frisby's first visit to Mr. Ages?

2. What convinces Mrs. Frisby to go see the owl?

3. Why is Timothy not told his mother is going to see the owl?

4. How do the rats get the powder into Dragon's dish?

5. After the men catch the rats, what do they say about the rats and their ability to communicate?

6. According to Nicodemus, what do the rats eventually learn after their initial fear and uncertainty?

7. How does Dr. Schultz organize the rats?

8. What happens after Nicodemus runs the Maze more often? Why does he still run through it?

9. What were the injections doing to Group A?

10. How did Justin get out of his cage after the doctor and his assistants went home for the night?

11. What did the rats do late into the night all winter long while staying at the Boniface Estate?

12. What is "The Plan"?

13. What happened at Henderson's Hardware Store?

14. What are some of the things the rats did in order to move Mrs. Frisby's house?

15. What do the seven rats do to trick the exterminators?

IV. Composition
1. Choose two different alternate titles for the book and explain your choices fully.

2. Is *Mrs. Frisby and the Rats of NIMH* more than just an adventure story? Why or why not?

3. Explain how The Plan is central to the meaning of the story.

4. Where is the climax of the story? Support your choice.

V. Vocabulary

Write the vocabulary words you are given. After writing them down, go back and write in their definitions.

Word	Definition
1	
2	
3	
4	
5	
6	
7	
8	
9	
10	

Mrs. Frisby And The Rats Of NIMH Short Answer Unit Test 2 Answer Key

I. Matching

A	1.	PNEUMONIA	A.	Timothy's illness
J	2.	BUSH	B.	Paul thinks the Public Health Service is investigating this disease in rats.
E	3.	SHREW	C.	Rats get this through the maze floor when they go the wrong way.
M	4.	ELECTROCUTED	D.	Billy uses it as a rat trap.
H	5.	TWENTY	E.	Mrs. Frisby's neighbor
P	6.	MOVING	F.	____ RATS INVADE HARDWARE STORE
I	7.	LIBRARY	G.	The men said they could capture the rats because they had become ___.
N	8.	THREE	H.	Number of rats that escaped from NIMH
S	9.	READING	I.	Where Mrs. Frisby waits for her first meeting with Nicodemus
Q	10.	MOUNTAINS	J.	Thorny covering over the entrance to the rat hole: rose ____
L	11.	TOOLS	K.	They tell Nicodemus to go to the owl.
K	12.	CHIPMUNKS	L.	The real treasure the rats find in the Toy Tinker's truck
D	13.	COLANDER	M.	Jenner and his group were ___ when trying to steal a motor.
B	14.	RABIES	N.	Number of rat groups in the NIMH lab
R	15.	OWL	O.	The Plan is to learn to live without ___.
G	16.	CARELESS	P.	Mrs. Frisby worries about this while Timothy is sick: ___ Day
C	17.	SHOCK	Q.	National Forest where the rats decide to move while at Boniface: Thorn ___
T	18.	WRITE	R.	The oldest animal in the woods who gives advice
O	19.	STEALING	S.	Most important skill the rats learn in NIMH
F	20.	MECHANIZED	T.	The rats spent their time reading and learning to ___ at Boniface Estate.

II. Identify

I	1.	JONATHAN	A.	Cat that killed Jonathan Frisby
J	2.	JEREMY	B.	Huge rat revived after breathing the gas
D	3.	AGES	C.	Male assistant in the NIMH lab
K	4.	FITZGIBBON	D.	He makes powders and potions.
O	5.	JENNER	E.	Doctor who runs NIMH
A	6.	DRAGON	F.	Helps Mrs. Frisby escape from Billy's cage
L	7.	ISABELLA	G.	He captures Mrs. Frisby under a colander.
B	8.	BRUTUS	H.	Yellow canary, once the Fitzgibbons' pet
F	9.	JUSTIN	I.	Mrs. Frisby's husband
E	10.	SCHULTZ	J.	He takes Mrs. Frisby to see the owl.
C	11.	GEORGE	K.	The farmer
G	12.	BILLY	L.	Young female rat Mrs. Frisby encounters in the library
M	13.	JULIE	M.	Dr. Schultz's female assistant
N	14.	FRISBY	N.	She puts the sleeping powder in the cat's bowl.
H	15.	PORGY	O.	Nicodemus's best friend growing up

III. Short Answer
1. What was the purpose of Mrs. Frisby's first visit to Mr. Ages?
   Timothy wandered away while playing with the other children and was bitten by a poisonous spider. Mrs. Frisby and her husband carried him to Mr. Ages, who gave him a milky liquid to "unlock" his muscles and treat his symptoms.
2. What convinces Mrs. Frisby to go see the owl?
   She thinks of Timothy and the big plow blade. She tells herself she has no choice and if there is any chance that the owl might help her she must go.
3. Why is Timothy not told his mother is going to see the owl?
   Timothy is not told about the expedition lest he worry and blame himself for the risk his mother must take.
4. How do the rats get the powder into Dragon's dish?
   There is a very shallow space between the floor and the bottom of the cabinet in the Fitzgibbons' kitchen. There is a hole behind the cabinet that they previously cut. Mr. Ages usually crawls through the hole and underneath the cabinet, dashes out to Dragon's bowl, deposits the powder in his food, and dashes back through the hole.
5. After the men catch the rats, what do they say about the rats and their ability to communicate?
   One tells the others that the rats can communicate and will inform the others about their experience. He says the rats will case the place carefully before they come again, but they will not come for a few more days. He also says they are lucky to have caught so many. The rats had not been bothered in so long they had grown careless.
6. According to Nicodemus, what do the rats eventually learn after their initial fear and uncertainty?
   They learn that uncertainty is the worst thing they will undergo. They are treated very well, except for small, quick flashes of pain that are part of their training. They are always well fed, although the food is not delicious by any means.
7. How does Dr. Schultz organize the rats?
   He splits them up into groups A, B, and C. There are twenty in group A, twenty in group B, and 23 in group C. The cages and collars for the rats are numbered accordingly. The rats in the A group will receive injections of series A and training. The rats in B will receive injections of series B and training. Group C will be the control group and only receive a prick from a plain needle.
8. What happens after Nicodemus runs the Maze more often? Why does he still run through it?
   Each time Nicodemus runs through the Maze his completion time is shorter. Julie, George, or Dr. Schultz picks him up at the end of the maze and writes down his time. Nicodemus understands that he will never get away. He runs through the Maze because he lives in a cage and cannot bear not to run, even if he is running toward an illusion.
9. What were the injections doing to Group A?
   The rats were becoming smarter than rats had ever been before, and the aging process seemed to stop almost completely.
10. How did Justin get out of his cage after the doctor and his assistants went home for the night?
    Justin read the instructions on the bottom of the cage informing him how to open the door.
11. What did the rats do late into the night all winter long while staying at the Boniface Estate?
    They studied the books in the library and taught themselves to write.

12. What is "The Plan"?
    The Plan is to live without stealing.
13. What happened at Henderson's Hardware Store?
    Six or seven rats got themselves electrocuted there while trying to move a motor.
14. What are some of the things the rats did in order to move Mrs. Frisby's house?
    They used a scaffolding system and pulleys to lift the house. Then, they put round pieces of wood resembling sawed-off broom handles under the cinder block and rolled it like a truck to its new location. They also dug a hole precisely the size of the cinder block so that it would fit nicely in its new spot near the boulder. They used shovels to dig a new entrance to the house.
15. What do the seven rats do to trick the exterminators?
    They all run out at once. Then, they run out two or three at a time to make it look like dozens of rats are leaving the hole. In reality, most of the rats had left early in the morning.

V. Vocabulary
Write the vocabulary words you are given. After writing them down, go back and write in their definitions.

Word	Definition
1	
2	
3	
4	
5	
6	
7	
8	
9	
10	

Mrs. Frisby And The Rats Of NIMH Advanced Short Answer Unit Test

I. Matching/Identify

____ 1.	JEREMY	A.	The farmer
____ 2.	AGES	B.	Helps Mrs. Frisby escape from Billy's cage
____ 3.	FITZGIBBON	C.	Nicodemus's best friend growing up
____ 4.	NICODEMUS	D.	Dr. Schultz's female assistant
____ 5.	JENNER	E.	Cat that killed Jonathan Frisby
____ 6.	DRAGON	F.	She puts the sleeping powder in the cat's bowl.
____ 7.	ISABELLA	G.	Doctor who runs NIMH
____ 8.	BRUTUS	H.	Male assistant in the NIMH lab
____ 9.	JUSTIN	I.	Huge rat revived after breathing the gas
____ 10.	SCHULTZ	J.	Leader of the rat colony
____ 11.	GEORGE	K.	He takes Mrs. Frisby to see the owl.
____ 12.	BILLY	L.	He captures Mrs. Frisby under a colander.
____ 13.	JULIE	M.	He makes powders and potions.
____ 14.	FRISBY	N.	Yellow canary, once the Fitzgibbons' pet
____ 15.	PORGY	O.	Young female rat Mrs. Frisby encounters in the library

II. Short Answer
1. From what point of view is the story told? Why is that important?

2. What are two main conflicts in the story? Are they resolved? If so, how? If not, why not?

3. What are three main themes presented in *Mrs. Frisby and the Rats of NIMH*? Briefly describe each in a sentence or two.

4. Choose two different alternate titles for the book and explain your choices fully.

5. Compare and contrast Nicodemus and Jenner.

6. How are the animal characters in the story different from humans? How are they the same?

7. Describe the relationship between the animals and Mr. Fitzgibbon.

8. Which character in the book is the least honorable? Most honorable? Justify your answer.

9. What did the fact that the rats made The Plan say about them?

10. Where is the climax of the story? Support your choice.

III. Essay
1. Write a letter to Dr. Schultz either persuading him to stop his experiments or encouraging him to continue them, based on your knowledge of Nicodemus's group. Use specific facts from the story to support your points.

IV. Vocabulary
   A. Write the vocabulary words you are given. After writing them down, go back and write in their definitions.

Word	Definition
1	
2	
3	
4	
5	
6	
7	
8	
9	
10	

   B. Write a short paragraph using 8 of these 10 words.

Mrs. Frisby And The Rats Of NIMH Advanced Short Answer Unit Test Answer Key

I. Matching/Identify

K	1.	JEREMY	A.	The farmer
M	2.	AGES	B.	Helps Mrs. Frisby escape from Billy's cage
A	3.	FITZGIBBON	C.	Nicodemus's best friend growing up
J	4.	NICODEMUS	D.	Dr. Schultz's female assistant
C	5.	JENNER	E.	Cat that killed Jonathan Frisby
E	6.	DRAGON	F.	She puts the sleeping powder in the cat's bowl.
O	7.	ISABELLA	G.	Doctor who runs NIMH
I	8.	BRUTUS	H.	Male assistant in the NIMH lab
B	9.	JUSTIN	I.	Huge rat revived after breathing the gas
G	10.	SCHULTZ	J.	Leader of the rat colony
H	11.	GEORGE	K.	He takes Mrs. Frisby to see the owl.
L	12.	BILLY	L.	He captures Mrs. Frisby under a colander.
D	13.	JULIE	M.	He makes powders and potions.
F	14.	FRISBY	N.	Yellow canary, once the Fitzgibbons' pet
N	15.	PORGY	O.	Young female rat Mrs. Frisby encounters in the library

Mrs. Frisby And The Rats Of NIMH Multiple Choice Unit Test 1

I. Identify

____ 1. JONATHAN   A. Yellow canary, once the Fitzgibbons' pet

____ 2. JEREMY   B. He takes Mrs. Frisby to see the owl.

____ 3. AGES   C. She puts the sleeping powder in the cat's bowl.

____ 4. FITZGIBBON   D. Leader of the rat colony

____ 5. NICODEMUS   E. The farmer

____ 6. JENNER   F. Young female rat Mrs. Frisby encounters in the library

____ 7. ISABELLA   G. Huge rat revived after breathing the gas

____ 8. BRUTUS   H. Doctor who runs NIMH

____ 9. JUSTIN   I. Mrs. Frisby's husband

____ 10. SCHULTZ   J. Male assistant in the NIMH lab

____ 11. GEORGE   K. Helps Mrs. Frisby escape from Billy's cage

____ 12. PAUL   L. Nicodemus's best friend growing up

____ 13. BILLY   M. He captures Mrs. Frisby under a colander.

____ 14. FRISBY   N. Farmer Fitzgibbon's oldest son

____ 15. PORGY   O. He makes powders and potions.

II. Matching

____ 1. BUSH A. Jenner and his group were ___ when trying to steal a motor.
____ 2. THORN B. The men said they could capture the rats because they had become ___.
____ 3. ELECTROCUTED C. Mrs. Frisby's house needs to be moved to the ___ of the stone.
____ 4. BONIFACE D. ____ RATS INVADE HARDWARE STORE
____ 5. TWENTY E. Number of rats that escaped from NIMH
____ 6. LEE F. Thorny covering over the entrance to the rat hole: rose ____
____ 7. PLAN G. The Plan is to learn to live without ___.
____ 8. THREE H. The real treasure the rats find in the Toy Tinker's truck
____ 9. MAZE I. They tell Nicodemus to go to the owl.
____ 10. READING J. Completion of it would eliminate stealing: The ___
____ 11. EIGHT K. Most important skill the rats learn in NIMH
____ 12. TOOLS L. Estate where the rats stayed after NIMH
____ 13. CHIPMUNKS M. Number of rat groups in the NIMH lab
____ 14. CAPACITY N. Isabella thinks Mrs. Frisby is one.
____ 15. SPY O. The rats spent their time reading and learning to ___ at Boniface Estate.
____ 16. CARELESS P. Set of corridors Nicodemus ran through while George watched
____ 17. THREAD Q. The rats used this when exploring the ducts.
____ 18. WRITE R. The size of an animal's brain is no measure of its ___.
____ 19. STEALING S. Place Nicodemus wants to move the rat colony: ___ Valley
____ 20. MECHANIZED T. Number of mice the rats free from their cages

III. Multiple Choice

1. Mrs. Frisby worries about all of the following on her trip to Mr. Ages EXCEPT:
   A. The long, risky journey
   B. The farmer's cat
   C. The sun going down
   D. The farmer's dog

2. Who says that the size of an animal's brain is no measure of its capacity?
   A. Mrs. Frisby
   B. The Lady Shrew
   C. Jeremy
   D. Mr. Frisby

3. What convinces Mrs. Frisby to go see the owl?
   A. She sees Dragon lurking nearby.
   B. The sun warms her, and she knows the frost will soon be gone.
   C. She remembered that Mr. Frisby used to say, "Nothing ventured, nothing gained."
   D. She thinks of Timothy and the big plow blade.

4. What does "in the lee" mean?
   A. In trouble
   B. Having plenty of what one needs
   C. Going a good way; following a good course of action
   D. On the calm side, the side the wind does not blow from

5. Why doesn't Dragon follow animals into the rose bush?
   A. The thorns deter him.
   B. Mrs. Fitzgibbon will beat him if she sees him in the bush.
   C. Following the animals into the bush would be too undignified.
   D. He is afraid of it.

6. Why does Mrs. Frisby decide against leaving the library to look around?
   A. Nicodemus told her to wait in the library. She doesn't want to pry; she is there for help.
   B. The library doors were too heavy for her to push open. She decided to give up trying to open them.
   C. She sees Justin watching the library door from down the hall.
   D. She was afraid she would get lost.

7. What does Mrs. Frisby learn from Isabella about the rat colony?
    A. They are plotting against Dragon.
    B. They are ill.
    C. Jenner did not like the Plan and deserted.
    D. They are building a new home in the forest.

8. Where do the men take Nicodemus, Jenner, and the other rats?
    A. To a laboratory
    B. To a warehouse
    C. To the farm
    D. To a pet store

9. According to Nicodemus, why does Dr. Schultz keep the rats in captivity?
    A. To test a serum and see if it makes them smarter
    B. To breed more rats
    C. To test new kinds of rat food
    D. To observe how rats behave in captivity

10. What were the injections doing to Group A?
    A. The injections were slowly killing them.
    B. The rats were becoming smarter and stopped aging.
    C. The rats were becoming fatter and stronger.
    D. The rats were becoming better listeners.

11. How did Justin get out of his cage after the doctor and his assistants went home for the night?
    A. He read the instructions on the bottom of the cage.
    B. His cage door had not been closed properly.
    C. Nicodemus helped him open the cage door.
    D. Jenner helped him open the cage door.

12. What is "The Plan"?
    A. To live without stealing
    B. To live without fighting
    C. To live exactly as people do
    D. To live without fear

13. Why are rats the most hated animals on earth, according to Nicodemus?
    A. They look evil.
    B. They are filthy.
    C. They steal.
    D. They carry diseases.

14. Why didn't Jonathan Frisby tell his wife about NIMH?
    A. He was sworn to secrecy.
    B. He didn't want to take a chance on hurting her with the news.
    C. He didn't see any point in telling her since it couldn't be changed.
    D. He didn't want her to think he was abnormal or freakish.

15. Why do the rats want to destroy the machinery and the other conveniences of their current home?
    A. They don't want other animals to use it.
    B. It was all made with stolen materials.
    C. They don't want it to be discovered.
    D. They regret having made it.

16. What happens to Mrs. Frisby after she puts the sleeping draught into Dragon's bowl?
    A. Billy Fitzgibbon traps her under a colander.
    B. She realizes Mrs. Fitzgibbon has unknowingly blocked her exit, and she has nowhere to go.
    C. She becomes very sleepy and realizes she has inhaled too much of the dusty powder.
    D. Dragon chases her, and she gets lost.

17. What happened at Henderson's Hardware Store?
    A. Mr. Henderson killed six or seven rats he found in the store.
    B. Mr. Henderson had a heart attack.
    C. Mr. Henderson found mice stealing a motor.
    D. Six or seven rats were electrocuted.

18. Why does Brutus come to find Mrs. Frisby?
    A. Nicodemus wants to see her.
    B. Isabella misses her.
    C. Mr. Ages wants to see her.
    D. Justin wants to see her.

19. What did the rats do to make the exterminators believe it was an ordinary rat hole?
    A. They invited ordinary rats to act as decoys.
    B. They burned all the evidence of an advanced civilization.
    C. They gnawed through all the carpet, water pipes, and electric wires.
    D. They moved all the equipment to the cave and brought in garbage.

20. Why does Mrs. Frisby decide to tell the children about NIMH?
    A. Nicodemus told her to do so.
    B. She thought it would make a good bedtime story.
    C. She can't keep a secret.
    D. She believes they have a right to know because they might be different from other mice.

IV. Composition
1. What are three main themes presented in *Mrs. Frisby and the Rats of NIMH*? Briefly describe each in a sentence or two.

2. What did the fact that the rats made The Plan say about them?

3. Write a speech for Nicodemus to give to a group of ordinary rats, based on your knowledge of his character and his beliefs.

V. Vocabulary

____ 1. VIGOROUS   A. Such that cannot be moved or influenced by persuasion
____ 2. RESPITE   B. In a manner that is mysterious or obscure in meaning
____ 3. CORDIAL   C. Furnace or apparatus for burning materials
____ 4. ASTONISHED   D. A break
____ 5. HARROW   E. Mildly scolded; spoken to in disapproval
____ 6. INCINERATOR   F. Having or showing a clever or shrewd mind
____ 7. INEXTRICABLY   G. In a manner incapable of being disentangled
____ 8. INKLING   H. Bits and pieces of rubbish; litter
____ 9. UNERRINGLY   I. Agricultural implement with spike-like teeth or upright disks, for leveling and breaking-up clods in plowed land
____ 10. ASTUTE   J. Filled with sudden, overpowering surprise or wonder
____ 11. CONSTERNATION   K. Position that provides a clear, broad view
____ 12. DEBRIS   L. Strong; active; robust
____ 13. VENTILATION   M. In a manner expressing great anger or scorn
____ 14. ADMONISHED   N. Courteous; gracious; friendly
____ 15. INDIGNANTLY   O. A system that circulates air
____ 16. IMPASSE   P. Great fear or shock that makes one feel helpless
____ 17. DESPAIRINGLY   Q. A vague idea or notion
____ 18. CRYPTICALLY   R. A situation offering no escape
____ 19. VANTAGE   S. In a manner feeling or showing hopelessness
____ 20. INEXORABLE   T. Without mistakes

Mrs. Frisby And The Rats Of NIMH Multiple Choice Unit Test 1 Answer Key

I. Identify

I	1.	JONATHAN	A.	Yellow canary, once the Fitzgibbons' pet
B	2.	JEREMY	B.	He takes Mrs. Frisby to see the owl.
O	3.	AGES	C.	She puts the sleeping powder in the cat's bowl.
E	4.	FITZGIBBON	D.	Leader of the rat colony
D	5.	NICODEMUS	E.	The farmer
L	6.	JENNER	F.	Young female rat Mrs. Frisby encounters in the library
F	7.	ISABELLA	G.	Huge rat revived after breathing the gas
G	8.	BRUTUS	H.	Doctor who runs NIMH
K	9.	JUSTIN	I.	Mrs. Frisby's husband
H	10.	SCHULTZ	J.	Male assistant in the NIMH lab
J	11.	GEORGE	K.	Helps Mrs. Frisby escape from Billy's cage
N	12.	PAUL	L.	Nicodemus's best friend growing up
M	13.	BILLY	M.	He captures Mrs. Frisby under a colander.
C	14.	FRISBY	N.	Farmer Fitzgibbon's oldest son
A	15.	PORGY	O.	He makes powders and potions.

II. Matching

Answer	#	Term		Clue
F	1.	BUSH	A.	Jenner and his group were ___ when trying to steal a motor.
S	2.	THORN	B.	The men said they could capture the rats because they had become ___.
A	3.	ELECTROCUTED	C.	Mrs. Frisby's house needs to be moved to the ___ of the stone.
L	4.	BONIFACE	D.	____ RATS INVADE HARDWARE STORE
E	5.	TWENTY	E.	Number of rats that escaped from NIMH
C	6.	LEE	F.	Thorny covering over the entrance to the rat hole: rose ____
J	7.	PLAN	G.	The Plan is to learn to live without ___.
M	8.	THREE	H.	The real treasure the rats find in the Toy Tinker's truck
P	9.	MAZE	I.	They tell Nicodemus to go to the owl.
K	10.	READING	J.	Completion of it would eliminate stealing: The ___
T	11.	EIGHT	K.	Most important skill the rats learn in NIMH
H	12.	TOOLS	L.	Estate where the rats stayed after NIMH
I	13.	CHIPMUNKS	M.	Number of rat groups in the NIMH lab
R	14.	CAPACITY	N.	Isabella thinks Mrs. Frisby is one.
N	15.	SPY	O.	The rats spent their time reading and learning to ___ at Boniface Estate.
B	16.	CARELESS	P.	Set of corridors Nicodemus ran through while George watched
Q	17.	THREAD	Q.	The rats used this when exploring the ducts.
O	18.	WRITE	R.	The size of an animal's brain is no measure of its ___.
G	19.	STEALING	S.	Place Nicodemus wants to move the rat colony: ___ Valley
D	20.	MECHANIZED	T.	Number of mice the rats free from their cages

III. Multiple Choice

B 1. Mrs. Frisby worries about all of the following on her trip to Mr. Ages EXCEPT:
- A. The long, risky journey
- B. The farmer's cat
- C. The sun going down
- D. The farmer's dog

D 2. Who says that the size of an animal's brain is no measure of its capacity?
- A. Mrs. Frisby
- B. The Lady Shrew
- C. Jeremy
- D. Mr. Frisby

D 3. What convinces Mrs. Frisby to go see the owl?
- A. She sees Dragon lurking nearby.
- B. The sun warms her, and she knows the frost will soon be gone.
- C. She remembered that Mr. Frisby used to say, "Nothing ventured, nothing gained."
- D. She thinks of Timothy and the big plow blade.

D 4. What does "in the lee" mean?
- A. In trouble
- B. Having plenty of what one needs
- C. Going a good way; following a good course of action
- D. On the calm side, the side the wind does not blow from

A 5. Why doesn't Dragon follow animals into the rose bush?
- A. The thorns deter him.
- B. Mrs. Fitzgibbon will beat him if she sees him in the bush.
- C. Following the animals into the bush would be too undignified.
- D. He is afraid of it.

A 6. Why does Mrs. Frisby decide against leaving the library to look around?
- A. Nicodemus told her to wait in the library. She doesn't want to pry; she is there for help.
- B. The library doors were too heavy for her to push open. She decided to give up trying to open them.
- C. She sees Justin watching the library door from down the hall.
- D. She was afraid she would get lost.

C 7. What does Mrs. Frisby learn from Isabella about the rat colony?
- A. They are plotting against Dragon.
- B. They are ill.
- C. Jenner did not like the Plan and deserted.
- D. They are building a new home in the forest.

A 8. Where do the men take Nicodemus, Jenner, and the other rats?
- A. To a laboratory
- B. To a warehouse
- C. To the farm
- D. To a pet store

A 9. According to Nicodemus, why does Dr. Schultz keep the rats in captivity?
- A. To test a serum and see if it makes them smarter
- B. To breed more rats
- C. To test new kinds of rat food
- D. To observe how rats behave in captivity

B 10. What were the injections doing to Group A?
- A. The injections were slowly killing them.
- B. The rats were becoming smarter and stopped aging.
- C. The rats were becoming fatter and stronger.
- D. The rats were becoming better listeners.

A 11. How did Justin get out of his cage after the doctor and his assistants went home for the night?
- A. He read the instructions on the bottom of the cage.
- B. His cage door had not been closed properly.
- C. Nicodemus helped him open the cage door.
- D. Jenner helped him open the cage door.

A 12. What is "The Plan"?
- A. To live without stealing
- B. To live without fighting
- C. To live exactly as people do
- D. To live without fear

C 13. Why are rats the most hated animals on earth, according to Nicodemus?
- A. They look evil.
- B. They are filthy.
- C. They steal.
- D. They carry diseases.

B 14. Why didn't Jonathan Frisby tell his wife about NIMH?
- A. He was sworn to secrecy.
- B. He didn't want to take a chance on hurting her with the news.
- C. He didn't see any point in telling her since it couldn't be changed.
- D. He didn't want her to think he was abnormal or freakish.

C 15. Why do the rats want to destroy the machinery and the other conveniences of their current home?
- A. They don't want other animals to use it.
- B. It was all made with stolen materials.
- C. They don't want it to be discovered.
- D. They regret having made it.

A 16. What happens to Mrs. Frisby after she puts the sleeping draught into Dragon's bowl?
- A. Billy Fitzgibbon traps her under a colander.
- B. She realizes Mrs. Fitzgibbon has unknowingly blocked her exit, and she has nowhere to go.
- C. She becomes very sleepy and realizes she has inhaled too much of the dusty powder.
- D. Dragon chases her, and she gets lost.

D 17. What happened at Henderson's Hardware Store?
- A. Mr. Henderson killed six or seven rats he found in the store.
- B. Mr. Henderson had a heart attack.
- C. Mr. Henderson found mice stealing a motor.
- D. Six or seven rats were electrocuted.

A 18. Why does Brutus come to find Mrs. Frisby?
- A. Nicodemus wants to see her.
- B. Isabella misses her.
- C. Mr. Ages wants to see her.
- D. Justin wants to see her.

D 19. What did the rats do to make the exterminators believe it was an ordinary rat hole?
- A. They invited ordinary rats to act as decoys.
- B. They burned all the evidence of an advanced civilization.
- C. They gnawed through all the carpet, water pipes, and electric wires.
- D. They moved all the equipment to the cave and brought in garbage.

D 20. Why does Mrs. Frisby decide to tell the children about NIMH?
- A. Nicodemus told her to do so.
- B. She thought it would make a good bedtime story.
- C. She can't keep a secret.
- D. She believes they have a right to know because they might be different from other mice.

V. Vocabulary

L	1.	VIGOROUS	A.	Such that cannot be moved or influenced by persuasion
D	2.	RESPITE	B.	In a manner that is mysterious or obscure in meaning
N	3.	CORDIAL	C.	Furnace or apparatus for burning materials
J	4.	ASTONISHED	D.	A break
I	5.	HARROW	E.	Mildly scolded; spoken to in disapproval
C	6.	INCINERATOR	F.	Having or showing a clever or shrewd mind
G	7.	INEXTRICABLY	G.	In a manner incapable of being disentangled
Q	8.	INKLING	H.	Bits and pieces of rubbish; litter
T	9.	UNERRINGLY	I.	Agricultural implement with spike-like teeth or upright disks, for leveling and breaking-up clods in plowed land
F	10.	ASTUTE	J.	Filled with sudden, overpowering surprise or wonder
P	11.	CONSTERNATION	K.	Position that provides a clear, broad view
H	12.	DEBRIS	L.	Strong; active; robust
O	13.	VENTILATION	M.	In a manner expressing great anger or scorn
E	14.	ADMONISHED	N.	Courteous; gracious; friendly
M	15.	INDIGNANTLY	O.	A system that circulates air
R	16.	IMPASSE	P.	Great fear or shock that makes one feel helpless
S	17.	DESPAIRINGLY	Q.	A vague idea or notion
B	18.	CRYPTICALLY	R.	A situation offering no escape
K	19.	VANTAGE	S.	In a manner feeling or showing hopelessness
A	20.	INEXORABLE	T.	Without mistakes

Mrs. Frisby And The Rats Of NIMH Multiple Choice Unit Test 2

I. Matching/Identify

____ 1.	JEREMY	A.	Huge rat revived after breathing the gas
____ 2.	AGES	B.	Mrs. Frisby's house needs to be moved to the ___ of the stone.
____ 3.	DRAGON	C.	National Forest where the rats decide to move while at Boniface: Thorn ___
____ 4.	BRUTUS	D.	Number of rat groups in the NIMH lab
____ 5.	JUSTIN	E.	Billy uses it as a rat trap.
____ 6.	SCHULTZ	F.	Helps Mrs. Frisby escape from Billy's cage
____ 7.	GEORGE	G.	The Plan is to learn to live without ___.
____ 8.	BILLY	H.	Doctor who runs NIMH
____ 9.	LEE	I.	He captures Mrs. Frisby under a colander.
____ 10.	PLAN	J.	Farming tool Nicodemus designs for the rats to use
____ 11.	THREE	K.	Cat that killed Jonathan Frisby
____ 12.	READING	L.	Completion of it would eliminate stealing: The ___
____ 13.	EIGHT	M.	Isabella thinks Mrs. Frisby is one.
____ 14.	PLOW	N.	He takes Mrs. Frisby to see the owl.
____ 15.	MOUNTAINS	O.	He makes powders and potions.
____ 16.	FRISBY	P.	Most important skill the rats learn in NIMH
____ 17.	COLANDER	Q.	The rats spent their time reading and learning to ___ at Boniface Estate.
____ 18.	SPY	R.	Male assistant in the NIMH lab
____ 19.	WRITE	S.	She puts the sleeping powder in the cat's bowl.
____ 20.	STEALING	T.	Number of mice the rats free from their cages

II. Multiple Choice

1. Which of these is a symptom of Timothy's illness?
   A. Shortness of breath
   B. Sneezing
   C. Stomach pain
   D. Muscle aches

2. According to Nicodemus, what do the rats eventually learn after their initial fear and uncertainty after their capture?
   A. The men are trying to get the rats to fight among themselves.
   B. Their worst fears will be confirmed; they will all die.
   C. Uncertainty is the worst thing they will undergo.
   D. Cats are allowed in the room at night, to guard the cages.

3. How are the rats in Group C different from A and B?
   A. They are the older rats.
   B. They are the control group; they receive no injections.
   C. They are the youngest rats.
   D. They receive injections of the "smart" serum.

4. What were Dr. Schultz and his assistants attempting to do when they showed the rats a picture of a rat and symbols while playing a recording that said "Are, Aie, Tea, Rat"?
   A. They were teaching the rats to sing.
   B. They were teaching the rats nonsense words.
   C. They were teaching the rats to read.
   D. They were teaching the rats to listen.

5. Which of the following is NOT a reason Justin didn't want Nicodemus to explore the laboratory with him?
   A. Justin was being cautious.
   B. Nicodemus was sleeping, and Justin didn't want to disturb him.
   C. Justin didn't want Nicodemus to get into trouble.
   D. Justin thought if the two of them got caught the doctors would know how smart the rats had become.

6. What did the rats do late into the night all winter long while staying at the Boniface Estate?
   A. The rats learned to cook.
   B. The rats studied books and practiced writing.
   C. The rats built machines.
   D. The rats played games like the old days before NIMH.

7. What is "The Plan"?
   A. To live exactly as people do
   B. To live without fighting
   C. To live without stealing
   D. To live without fear

8. Describe what Nicodemus and the rats found in the Toy Tinker's truck.
   A. A box with NIMH printed on the side
   B. A huge stash of food
   C. Mechanical rats
   D. Tools small enough for the rats to use

9. Why doesn't Justin simply open the door of Mrs. Frisby's cage?
   A. Dragon is sitting in front of it.
   B. He can't; he isn't physically strong enough.
   C. He doesn't want Mr. Fitzgibbons to become suspicious.
   D. He can't reach it.

10. According to the man, why were they able to catch the rats?
    A. The rats were sleeping.
    B. The rats had grown careless.
    C. The rats were distracted.
    D. The rats were too tired to run away.

11. According to Nicodemus, what did the owl mean by moving Mrs. Frisby's house "in the lee" of the stone?
    A. The house should be in a carved-out area of the stone.
    B. The house should be under the rock.
    C. The house should be in close behind the rock where the plow does not reach.
    D. The house should be on top of the stone where Mrs. Frisby can see the plow coming.

12. What does Mrs. Frisby learn from Isabella about the rat colony?
    A. They are building a new home in the forest.
    B. They are plotting against Dragon.
    C. Jenner did not like the Plan and deserted.
    D. They are ill.

13. Mrs. Frisby worries about all of the following on her trip to Mr. Ages EXCEPT:
    A. The sun going down
    B. The farmer's dog
    C. The farmer's cat
    D. The long, risky journey

14. Who says that the size of an animal's brain is no measure of its capacity?
    A. Jeremy
    B. Mrs. Frisby
    C. The Lady Shrew
    D. Mr. Frisby

15. Why must all the animals move out of the garden when winter is over?
    A. They could be washed away in the spring rains.
    B. There is no shade for protection from the sun in the garden.
    C. Farmer Fitzgibbon's plow will run over them if they stay.
    D. The powders, fertilizers, and sprays used in the garden make the animals sick if they stay.

16. Why didn't the Frisbys make their winter home in the barn lofts or attics like some field mice?
    A. There wasn't enough room in the barn lofts and attics for all of the animals.
    B. The Frisbys preferred the relative safety and freedom of the outdoors.
    C. The Frisbys didn't know about the lofts and attics.
    D. The garden had been the winter home of the Frisbys for generations; they couldn't give it up.

17. What is the owl's advice to Mrs. Frisby?
    A. To leave before he eats her
    B. To take a chance on moving Timothy to the house of her nearest relative
    C. To go home and stop bothering him
    D. To go see the rat Nicodemus

18. Mrs. Frisby is astonished by many things in the corridor of the rat hole. Which of these is NOT something that astonished her?
    A. Carpeting
    B. Green, blue, and yellow glass
    C. Recessed lighting
    D. Speakers playing music

19. Why does Mrs. Frisby decide against leaving the library to look around?
    A. Nicodemus told her to wait in the library. She doesn't want to pry; she is there for help.
    B. She was afraid she would get lost.
    C. She sees Justin watching the library door from down the hall.
    D. The library doors were too heavy for her to push open. She decided to give up trying to open them.

20. Who or what does Isabella think Mrs. Frisby is?
    A. An inspector
    B. An imposter
    C. A spy from the outside or from NIMH
    D. A thief trying to steal some of their provisions

21. Why does Mrs. Frisby decide to tell the children about NIMH?
    A. Nicodemus told her to do so.
    B. She thought it would make a good bedtime story.
    C. She believes they have a right to know because they might be different from other mice.
    D. She can't keep a secret.

III. Composition
1. How do you think Nicodemus would describe Jenner?

2. Choose three of the following characters and fully explain the purpose of each in the story: Dragon, Justin, Jeremy, the owl, Jonathan Frisby.

3. Who is the main character of *Mrs. Frisby and the Rats of NIMH*? Justify your answer.

4. Is the story of *Mrs. Frisby and the Rats of NIMH* believable? Why or why not?

5. Explain how The Plan is central to the meaning of the story.

6. Where is the climax of the story? Support your choice.

IV. Vocabulary

___ 1.	PROTRUDED	A.	Person who goes from place to place selling small articles
___ 2.	ILLOGICAL	B.	A very strong wind
___ 3.	VENTURED	C.	Came forth
___ 4.	AGITATED	D.	Making twisting or turning movements
___ 5.	YIELDED	E.	Slant upward
___ 6.	INCLINE	F.	Came together to meet at a point or in a line
___ 7.	SUBSIDING	G.	In a tired or worn-out manner
___ 8.	CONVERGED	H.	Becoming quieter or less active
___ 9.	EMERGED	I.	Dared to do something dangerous or risky
___ 10.	ASTUTE	J.	Make an earnest request
___ 11.	GALE	K.	Troubled or nervous
___ 12.	SKEPTICAL	L.	Stuck out; extended beyond
___ 13.	PEDDLER	M.	Prevalent and spreading rapidly among many individuals
___ 14.	CYNICAL	N.	Having or showing a clever or shrewd mind
___ 15.	PESSIMIST	O.	Doubtful; not easily persuaded or convinced
___ 16.	PLEAD	P.	Person who sees everything in a negative or the worst possible way
___ 17.	EPIDEMIC	Q.	Empty
___ 18.	WEARILY	R.	Believing that people are only motivated by selfishness
___ 19.	VACANT	S.	Contrary to or disregarding the rules of logic
___ 20.	WRITHING	T.	Gave way

Mrs. Frisby And The Rats Of NIMH Multiple Choice Unit Test 2 Answer Key

I. Matching/Identify

N	1.	JEREMY	A.	Huge rat revived after breathing the gas
O	2.	AGES	B.	Mrs. Frisby's house needs to be moved to the ___ of the stone.
K	3.	DRAGON	C.	National Forest where the rats decide to move while at Boniface: Thorn ___
A	4.	BRUTUS	D.	Number of rat groups in the NIMH lab
F	5.	JUSTIN	E.	Billy uses it as a rat trap.
H	6.	SCHULTZ	F.	Helps Mrs. Frisby escape from Billy's cage
R	7.	GEORGE	G.	The Plan is to learn to live without ___.
I	8.	BILLY	H.	Doctor who runs NIMH
B	9.	LEE	I.	He captures Mrs. Frisby under a colander.
L	10.	PLAN	J.	Farming tool Nicodemus designs for the rats to use
D	11.	THREE	K.	Cat that killed Jonathan Frisby
P	12.	READING	L.	Completion of it would eliminate stealing: The ___
T	13.	EIGHT	M.	Isabella thinks Mrs. Frisby is one.
J	14.	PLOW	N.	He takes Mrs. Frisby to see the owl.
C	15.	MOUNTAINS	O.	He makes powders and potions.
S	16.	FRISBY	P.	Most important skill the rats learn in NIMH
E	17.	COLANDER	Q.	The rats spent their time reading and learning to ___ at Boniface Estate.
M	18.	SPY	R.	Male assistant in the NIMH lab
Q	19.	WRITE	S.	She puts the sleeping powder in the cat's bowl.
G	20.	STEALING	T.	Number of mice the rats free from their cages

II. Multiple Choice

A 1. Which of these is a symptom of Timothy's illness?
   A. Shortness of breath
   B. Sneezing
   C. Stomach pain
   D. Muscle aches

C 2. According to Nicodemus, what do the rats eventually learn after their initial fear and uncertainty after their capture?
   A. The men are trying to get the rats to fight among themselves.
   B. Their worst fears will be confirmed; they will all die.
   C. Uncertainty is the worst thing they will undergo.
   D. Cats are allowed in the room at night, to guard the cages.

B 3. How are the rats in Group C different from A and B?
   A. They are the older rats.
   B. They are the control group; they receive no injections.
   C. They are the youngest rats.
   D. They receive injections of the "smart" serum.

C 4. What were Dr. Schultz and his assistants attempting to do when they showed the rats a picture of a rat and symbols while playing a recording that said "Are, Aie, Tea, Rat"?
   A. They were teaching the rats to sing.
   B. They were teaching the rats nonsense words.
   C. They were teaching the rats to read.
   D. They were teaching the rats to listen.

B 5. Which of the following is NOT a reason Justin didn't want Nicodemus to explore the laboratory with him?
   A. Justin was being cautious.
   B. Nicodemus was sleeping, and Justin didn't want to disturb him.
   C. Justin didn't want Nicodemus to get into trouble.
   D. Justin thought if the two of them got caught the doctors would know how smart the rats had become.

B 6. What did the rats do late into the night all winter long while staying at the Boniface Estate?
  A. The rats learned to cook.
  B. The rats studied books and practiced writing.
  C. The rats built machines.
  D. The rats played games like the old days before NIMH.

C 7. What is "The Plan"?
  A. To live exactly as people do
  B. To live without fighting
  C. To live without stealing
  D. To live without fear

D 8. Describe what Nicodemus and the rats found in the Toy Tinker's truck.
  A. A box with NIMH printed on the side
  B. A huge stash of food
  C. Mechanical rats
  D. Tools small enough for the rats to use

C 9. Why doesn't Justin simply open the door of Mrs. Frisby's cage?
  A. Dragon is sitting in front of it.
  B. He can't; he isn't physically strong enough.
  C. He doesn't want Mr. Fitzgibbons to become suspicious.
  D. He can't reach it.

B 10. According to the man, why were they able to catch the rats?
  A. The rats were sleeping.
  B. The rats had grown careless.
  C. The rats were distracted.
  D. The rats were too tired to run away.

C 11. According to Nicodemus, what did the owl mean by moving Mrs. Frisby's house "in the lee" of the stone?
  A. The house should be in a carved-out area of the stone.
  B. The house should be under the rock.
  C. The house should be in close behind the rock where the plow does not reach.
  D. The house should be on top of the stone where Mrs. Frisby can see the plow coming.

C 12. What does Mrs. Frisby learn from Isabella about the rat colony?
- A. They are building a new home in the forest.
- B. They are plotting against Dragon.
- C. Jenner did not like the Plan and deserted.
- D. They are ill.

C 13. Mrs. Frisby worries about all of the following on her trip to Mr. Ages EXCEPT:
- A. The sun going down
- B. The farmer's dog
- C. The farmer's cat
- D. The long, risky journey

D 14. Who says that the size of an animal's brain is no measure of its capacity?
- A. Jeremy
- B. Mrs. Frisby
- C. The Lady Shrew
- D. Mr. Frisby

C 15. Why must all the animals move out of the garden when winter is over?
- A. They could be washed away in the spring rains.
- B. There is no shade for protection from the sun in the garden.
- C. Farmer Fitzgibbon's plow will run over them if they stay.
- D. The powders, fertilizers, and sprays used in the garden make the animals sick if they stay.

B 16. Why didn't the Frisbys make their winter home in the barn lofts or attics like some field mice?
- A. There wasn't enough room in the barn lofts and attics for all of the animals.
- B. The Frisbys preferred the relative safety and freedom of the outdoors.
- C. The Frisbys didn't know about the lofts and attics.
- D. The garden had been the winter home of the Frisbys for generations; they couldn't give it up.

D 17.   What is the owl's advice to Mrs. Frisby?
   A. To leave before he eats her
   B. To take a chance on moving Timothy to the house of her nearest relative
   C. To go home and stop bothering him
   D. To go see the rat Nicodemus

D 18.   Mrs. Frisby is astonished by many things in the corridor of the rat hole. Which of these is NOT something that astonished her?
   A. Carpeting
   B. Green, blue, and yellow glass
   C. Recessed lighting
   D. Speakers playing music

A 19.   Why does Mrs. Frisby decide against leaving the library to look around?
   A. Nicodemus told her to wait in the library. She doesn't want to pry; she is there for help.
   B. She was afraid she would get lost.
   C. She sees Justin watching the library door from down the hall.
   D. The library doors were too heavy for her to push open. She decided to give up trying to open them.

C 20.   Who or what does Isabella think Mrs. Frisby is?
   A. An inspector
   B. An imposter
   C. A spy from the outside or from NIMH
   D. A thief trying to steal some of their provisions

C 21.   Why does Mrs. Frisby decide to tell the children about NIMH?
   A. Nicodemus told her to do so.
   B. She thought it would make a good bedtime story.
   C. She believes they have a right to know because they might be different from other mice.
   D. She can't keep a secret.

IV. Vocabulary

L	1.	PROTRUDED	A.	Person who goes from place to place selling small articles
S	2.	ILLOGICAL	B.	A very strong wind
I	3.	VENTURED	C.	Came forth
K	4.	AGITATED	D.	Making twisting or turning movements
T	5.	YIELDED	E.	Slant upward
E	6.	INCLINE	F.	Came together to meet at a point or in a line
H	7.	SUBSIDING	G.	In a tired or worn-out manner
F	8.	CONVERGED	H.	Becoming quieter or less active
C	9.	EMERGED	I.	Dared to do something dangerous or risky
N	10.	ASTUTE	J.	Make an earnest request
B	11.	GALE	K.	Troubled or nervous
O	12.	SKEPTICAL	L.	Stuck out; extended beyond
A	13.	PEDDLER	M.	Prevalent and spreading rapidly among many individuals
R	14.	CYNICAL	N.	Having or showing a clever or shrewd mind
P	15.	PESSIMIST	O.	Doubtful; not easily persuaded or convinced
J	16.	PLEAD	P.	Person who sees everything in a negative or the worst possible way
M	17.	EPIDEMIC	Q.	Empty
G	18.	WEARILY	R.	Believing that people are only motivated by selfishness
Q	19.	VACANT	S.	Contrary to or disregarding the rules of logic
D	20.	WRITHING	T.	Gave way

UNIT RESOURCE MATERIALS

BULLETIN BOARD IDEAS *Mrs. Frisby And The Rats Of NIMH*

1. Save one corner of the board for the best of students' *Mrs. Frisby and the Rats of NIMH* writing assignments.
2. Take one of the word search puzzles from the extra activities packet and with a marker copy it over in a large size on the bulletin board. Write the clue words to find to one side. Invite students prior to and after class to find the words and circle them on the bulletin board.
3. Write several of the most significant quotations from the book onto the board on brightly colored paper. Using string and thumb tacks, pin a few markers to the bulletin board for students to write their reflections about the quotations directly onto the bulletin board. Make sure to clarify what is and isn't appropriate language for a public bulletin board.
4. Make a bulletin board listing the vocabulary words for this unit. As you complete sections of the novel and discuss the vocabulary for each section, write the definitions on the bulletin board. (If your board is one students face frequently, it will help them learn the words.)
5. Post information about Ponce de Leon and the Fountain of Youth. Have students discuss the reason people are fascinated with prolonging life (like Dr. Schultz from the story).
6. Each day, have students predict what is going to happen in the next assignment and post the prediction on the board. Make sure to review the predictions after the assignment has been read.
7. Have students create a map of the farm and the surrounding area from Jeremy's point of view.
8. Have student draw a portrait of one of the characters and write a short description.
9. Make a bulletin board about the pros and cons of using animals for testing products and ideas.
10. The rats perceived their trait of theft as being the single most important thing to change about themselves. Have students consider what negative trait humans have that would be a good idea to change. Have each student make a small poster showing the trait and briefly outlining a Plan to fix the trait. Use the posters for your bulletin board titled "If We Could Change One Thing."
11. Make a bulletin board titled "A Good Place To Build A Home." Have students brainstorm qualities a good home site should have. Post pictures of homes in lots of different settings.

RELATED TOPICS *Mrs. Frisby And The Rats Of NIMH*

1. Farming/Gardening
2. Peddlers, past and present
3. Rats, Mice, Owls, Crows, Cats
4. Careers in Home Building or Moving
5. Moving
6. Home Building
7. Careers in Scientific Reserach
8. Careers in Energy Production or Management
9. Careers in Product Development
10. Careers in Agriculture
11. Self-Improvement
12. Fountain of Youth
13. Simple Machines
14. Evolution
15. Electricity
16. Animal Testing
17. Animal Rights
18. Hardware Stores--what they offer, how they've changed, careers

MORE ACTIVITIES *Mrs. Frisby And The Rats Of NIMH*

1. Have students work together to make a time line chronology of the events in the story. Take a large piece of construction paper and on one wall (or however you can physically arrange it in your room) and make the events of the story along it. Students may want to add drawings or cut-out pictures to represent the events (as well as a written statement).

2. Have students design a book cover (front and back and inside flaps) for *Mrs. Frisby and the Rats of NIMH*. I like to use a manila file folder for this activity because students can use it to store their pre-reading vocabulary worksheets and study guide questions. I also encourage students to keep any other worksheets, drawings, or compositions that they generate in the folder. It's just nice to have everything in one place!

3. Have students design a bulletin board (ready to be put up; not just sketched) for *Mrs. Frisby and the Rats of NIMH*.

4. Have students group the books together to show the larger structure of the novel. Have them explain why they chose the divisions they made.

5. Have students choose one chapter of the book (with sufficient dialogue) to rewrite as a play. In conjunction with this assignment, have students write a composition explaining the difficulties they encountered in changing from one written form to another. You may want to have students perform the play in class or film it at home in a small group.

6. Watch the movie *Mrs. Frisby and the Rats of NIMH* and compare it with the novel. Why might Michael Ende have disliked this movie? (He tried to have the production shut down and sued the filmmakers).

7. Have students write a song or a poem about a character, setting, or symbol in *Mrs. Frisby and the Rats of NIMH*. Ambitious students may even want to set the song to music.

8. Host a literary tea party in which students have a character taped to their back and they have to guess who it is based on conversations they have with other students

9. Mrs. Frisby saw her neighborhood (and beyond) from a different point of view when she flew with Jeremy. Go on the Internet with your students to Google Earth and look at your neighborhood from above! http://earth.google.com . If you haven't used Google Earth before, you'll need to download the software, so be sure to do this prior to class time. It's easy and fun!

10. Mrs. Frisby had to move her home. Take time to discuss with your students what is actually involved in moving a family. No doubt some of your students are already experienced movers. Brainstorm a list of all the things that must be done when a family moves.

11. We get a "behind the scenes" look at some of the animal life on Farmer Fitzgibon's farm. Have students brainstorm a list of animals that might live near their own homes and discuss what life might be like for those animals. You could add in a writing assignment for students to make a story from the point of view of an animal near their homes.

12. The rats recognized their worst trait was stealing. Have students stop and think about what their own personal worst trait might be, and have them write a Plan to fix it.

13. Mrs. Fitzgibbon apparently likes to garden. How many of your students have a garden? If not many do, take some time to talk about gardening, kinds of gardens, steps in creating and planting a garden, harvesting, care of plants, fertilizers, natural pest controls, and other related topics. If you have a large room with lots of sunshine, let each student plant something and harvest it. There are a whole range of writing and research assignments you could create around this project: daily journal with or without pictures, research the plant being grown, uses of the plant, a story involving the plant, etc.

14. If you are allowed, keep a pet mouse, rat, hampster, etc. in your room during this novel unit. You might see if any of your students or someone in the school already has such a pet you could borrow for a short time. Discuss the care of the animal and assign students specific tasks related to the care of the animal. You can create lots of writing assignments and activities related to this: research the animal, uses of the animal, a story involving the animal, a photo album with captions, a scrap book with each students' daily observations of the animal, a daily response journal, etc.

15. Show a DVD or have a guest speaker come talk about and demonstrate principles of electricity. Discuss what electricity added to the rats' lives and how our lives would be different without it. Discuss renewable energy sources and what the future might bring regarding energy use.

16. Have someone from a house moving company come to talk to your class--and hopefully bring some videos of actual buildings they have moved.

UNIT WORD LIST *Mrs. Frisby And The Rats Of NIMH*

No.	Word	Clue/Definition
1.	AGES	He makes powders and potions.
2.	AIR	Six of the mice were blown away by this in the duct.
3.	ARTHUR	Chief engineer of the rat colony
4.	BILLY	He captures Mrs. Frisby under a colander.
5.	BONIFACE	Estate where the rats stayed after NIMH
6.	BROOK	The Frisbys live near one in the summer.
7.	BRUTUS	Huge rat revived after breathing the gas
8.	BUSH	Thorny covering over the entrance to the rat hole: rose ____
9.	CAGE	Justin read instructions telling how to open the ___ door.
10.	CAPACITY	The size of an animal's brain is no measure of its ___.
11.	CARELESS	The men said they could capture the rats because they had become ___.
12.	CHIPMUNKS	They tell Nicodemus to go to the owl.
13.	CHRISTMAS	The rats stole most of their lights after this holiday.
14.	CIVILIZATION	Nicodemus wants the rats to build their own ___, like the Romans & others.
15.	COLANDER	Billy uses it as a rat trap.
16.	CONTROL	Group C was the ___ Group.
17.	DRAGON	Cat that killed Jonathan Frisby
18.	DUSK	Best time to talk to the owl
19.	EIGHT	Number of mice the rats free from their cages
20.	ELECTROCUTED	Jenner and his group were ___ when trying to steal a motor.
21.	EYE	Nicodemus has a patch over his left one.
22.	FITZGIBBON	The farmer
23.	FRISBY	She puts the sleeping powder in the cat's bowl.
24.	GEORGE	Male assistant in the NIMH lab
25.	GORDON	Owner of the Boniface Estate
26.	HENDERSON	Where Jenner and his group were stealing tools: ____'s Hardware
27.	HOUSE	The Frisbys must move theirs.
28.	ISABELLA	Young female rat Mrs. Frisby encounters in the library
29.	JENNER	Nicodemus's best friend growing up
30.	JEREMY	He takes Mrs. Frisby to see the owl.
31.	JONATHAN	Mrs. Frisby's husband
32.	JULIE	Dr. Schultz's female assistant
33.	JUSTIN	Helps Mrs. Frisby escape from Billy's cage
34.	LEE	Mrs. Frisby's house needs to be moved to the ___ of the stone.
35.	LIBRARY	Where Mrs. Frisby waits for her first meeting with Nicodemus
36.	MARTIN	Timothy's older brother

No.	Word	Clue/Definition
37.	MAZE	Set of corridors Nicodemus ran through while George watched
38.	MECHANIZED	___ RATS INVADE HARDWARE STORE
39.	MOUNTAINS	National Forest where the rats decide to move while at Boniface: Thorn ___
40.	MOVING	Mrs. Frisby worries about this while Timothy is sick: ___ Day
41.	NEUROLOGIST	Expert on brains, nerves, intelligence: Dr. Schultz is one
42.	NICODEMUS	Leader of the rat colony
43.	NIMH	Letters written on the truck when Nicodemus & Jenner were captured
44.	OWL	The oldest animal in the woods who gives advice
45.	PAUL	Farmer Fitzgibbon's oldest son
46.	PEOPLE	Nicodemus re-names the "rat race" to the "___ race."
47.	PIN	Part Farmer Fitzgibbon orders, which delays plowing: linch ___
48.	PLAN	Completion of it would eliminate stealing: The ___
49.	PLOW	Farming tool Nicodemus designs for the rats to use
50.	PNEUMONIA	Timothy's illness
51.	PORGY	Yellow canary, once the Fitzgibbons' pet
52.	POST	Location of Mrs. Frisby's hiding hole: fence ___
53.	RABIES	Paul thinks the Public Health Service is investigating this disease in rats.
54.	READING	Most important skill the rats learn in NIMH
55.	SCHULTZ	Doctor who runs NIMH
56.	SHOCK	Rats get this through the maze floor when they go the wrong way.
57.	SHREW	Mrs. Frisby's neighbor
58.	SPIDER	Creature that bit Timothy
59.	SPY	Isabella thinks Mrs. Frisby is one.
60.	STEALING	The Plan is to learn to live without ___.
61.	STUMP	Mrs. Frisby finds corn, nuts and mushrooms there.
62.	SULLIVAN	Rat who recommends plugging into the house current for electricity
63.	THORN	Place Nicodemus wants to move the rat colony: ___ Valley
64.	THREAD	The rats used this when exploring the ducts.
65.	THREE	Number of rat groups in the NIMH lab
66.	TOOLS	The real treasure the rats find in the Toy Tinker's truck
67.	TOY	Nicodemus & the rats found tools in his truck: ___ Tinker
68.	TRASH	The rats learned to remove ___ and clean the house to avoid being found.
69.	TWENTY	Number of rats that escaped from NIMH
70.	WRITE	The rats spent their time reading and learning to ___ at Boniface Estate.

WORD SEARCH Mrs. Frisby and the Rats of NIMH

```
T K A I N O M U E N P N D R A G O N Y T
O Y P Z F B C O L A N D E R N L I N K T
O T N K V E C S E D J U L I E T N L S S
L N Q P E H B H C F F Z D Z S O F B L V
S E L R O Z P Q T M F A F U D K W I A N
S W H L E S Y E R K E M J R Z K L L G X
T T U Y Y O T H O R N C O N T R O L E E
I A U J E I B O C P P G H U N R W Y S M
P S C M R F R S U N L L H A N O A P X C
N Q A W P B S U T E F E O R N T H S U B
I D R B C S C L E U I R R W A I A M H B
M F E D E A H L D R T G I P L B Z I Z V
H R L N I L U I A O Z S H S P Z I E N R
J W E R H S L V E L G H B T B M M E D S
V Q S A P Q T A R O I O R C A Y A G S J
F T S I R O Z N H G B C U R A R Z R H J
V P D P T T R W T I B K T D X G E O O S
N E V F I Q H G S S O I U U P H E E U K
R M O V I N G U Y T N Q S S W R G G S S
S Y L H E N D E R S O N P K J E N N E R
```

AGES	EYE	MOUNTAINS	SCHULTZ
AIR	FITZGIBBON	MOVING	SHOCK
ARTHUR	FRISBY	NEUROLOGIST	SHREW
BILLY	GEORGE	NIMH	SPIDER
BROOK	GORDON	OWL	SPY
BRUTUS	HENDERSON	PAUL	STUMP
BUSH	HOUSE	PEOPLE	SULLIVAN
CAGE	ISABELLA	PIN	THORN
CARELESS	JENNER	PLAN	THREAD
COLANDER	JULIE	PLOW	THREE
CONTROL	JUSTIN	PNEUMONIA	TOOLS
DRAGON	LEE	PORGY	TOY
DUSK	MARTIN	POST	TRASH
EIGHT	MAZE	RABIES	TWENTY
ELECTROCUTED	MECHANIZED	READING	WRITE

ANSWER KEY: WORD SEARCH Mrs. Frisby and the Rats of NIMH

AGES	EYE	MOUNTAINS	SCHULTZ
AIR	FITZGIBBON	MOVING	SHOCK
ARTHUR	FRISBY	NEUROLOGIST	SHREW
BILLY	GEORGE	NIMH	SPIDER
BROOK	GORDON	OWL	SPY
BRUTUS	HENDERSON	PAUL	STUMP
BUSH	HOUSE	PEOPLE	SULLIVAN
CAGE	ISABELLA	PIN	THORN
CARELESS	JENNER	PLAN	THREAD
COLANDER	JULIE	PLOW	THREE
CONTROL	JUSTIN	PNEUMONIA	TOOLS
DRAGON	LEE	PORGY	TOY
DUSK	MARTIN	POST	TRASH
EIGHT	MAZE	RABIES	TWENTY
ELECTROCUTED	MECHANIZED	READING	WRITE

CROSSWORD Mrs. Frisby and the Rats of NIMH

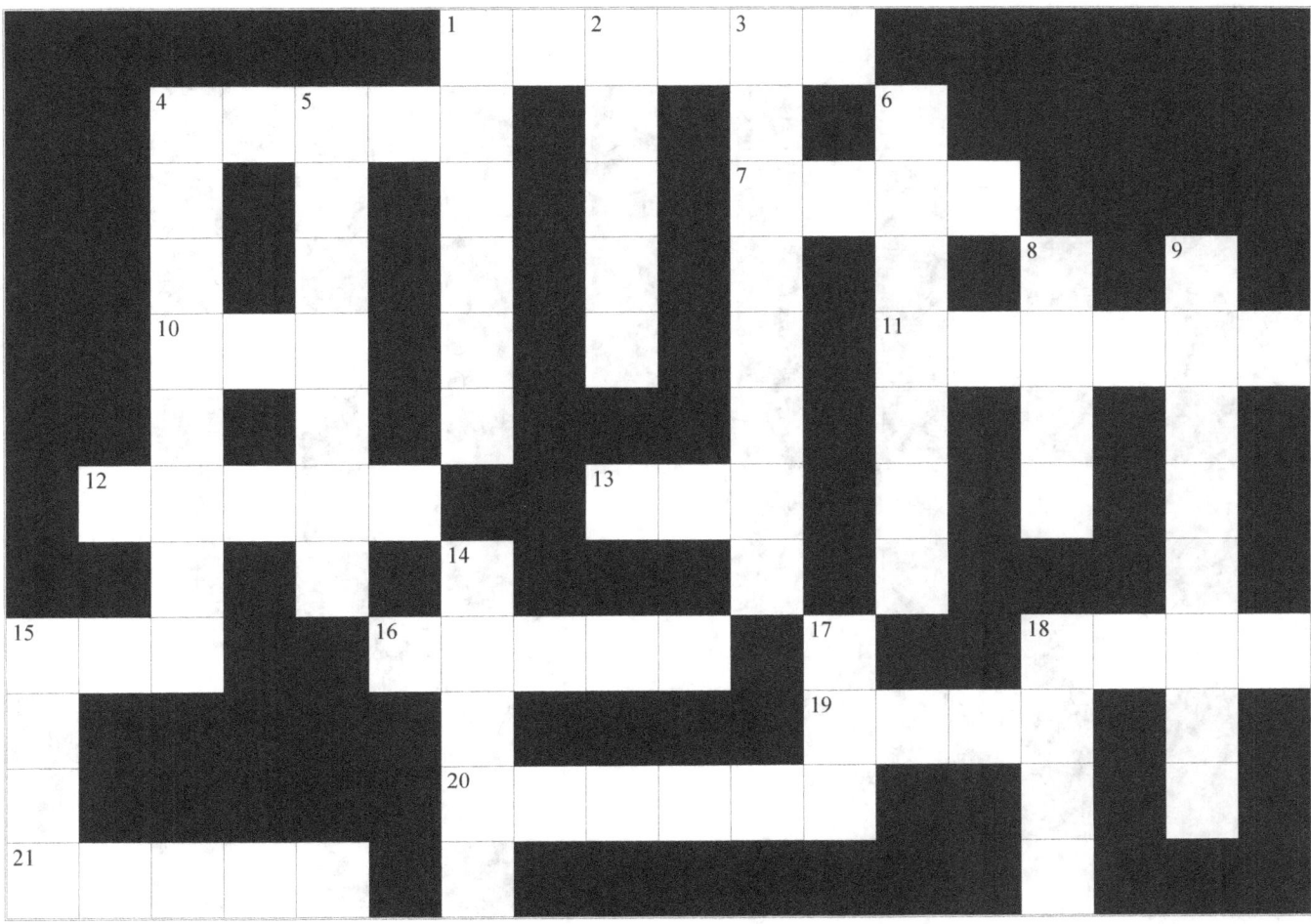

Across
1. He helps Mrs. Frisby escape from Billy.
4. Dr. Schultz's female assistant
7. He makes powders and potions.
10. Six of the mice were blown away by this in the duct.
11. Cat that killed Jonathan Frisby
12. Place Nicodemus wants to move the rat colony: ___ Valley
13. Oldest animal in the woods; he gives advice
15. Part Farmer Fitzgibbon orders, which delays plowing: linch ___
16. The Frisbys live near one in the summer.
18. Completion of it would eliminate stealing: The ___
19. Farmer Fitzgibbon's oldest son
20. Number of rats that escaped from NIMH
21. The real treasure the rats find in the Toy Tinker's truck

Down
1. Nicodemus's best friend growing up
2. Rats get this through the maze floor when they go the wrong way.
3. Young female rat Mrs. Frisby encounters in the library
4. Mrs. Frisby's husband; also one of the mice
5. Where Mrs. Frisby waits for her first meeting with Nicodemus.
6. Most important skill the rats learn in NIMH
8. Justin read instructions telling how to open the ___ door.
9. Estate where the rats stayed after NIMH
14. The rats spent their time reading and learning to ___ at Boniface Estate.
15. Location of Mrs. Frisby's hiding hole: fence ___
17. Isabella thinks Mrs. Frisby is one.
18. Farming tool Nicodemus designs for the rats to use

ANSWER KEY: CROSSWORD Mrs. Frisby and the Rats of NIMH

				1 J	2 U	3 S	T	I	N			
		4 J	5 U	L	I	E			6 R			
		O		I		N		7 A	G	E	S	
		N		B		N		B		A		8 C	9 B
		10 A	I	R		E		11 D	R	A	G	O	N
		T		A		R		I		G		N
	12 T	H	O	R	N		13 O	W	L			E		I
		A		Y		14 W		A					F
15 P	I	N			16 B	R	O	O	K		17 S		18 P	L	A	N
O					I					19 P	A	U	L		C
S					20 T	W	E	N	T	Y			O		E
21 T	O	O	L	S		E							W

Across
1. He helps Mrs. Frisby escape from Billy.
4. Dr. Schultz's female assistant
7. He makes powders and potions.
10. Six of the mice were blown away by this in the duct.
11. Cat that killed Jonathan Frisby
12. Place Nicodemus wants to move the rat colony: ___ Valley
13. Oldest animal in the woods; he gives advice
15. Part Farmer Fitzgibbon orders, which delays plowing: linch ___
16. The Frisbys live near one in the summer.
18. Completion of it would eliminate stealing: The ___
19. Farmer Fitzgibbon's oldest son
20. Number of rats that escaped from NIMH
21. The real treasure the rats find in the Toy Tinker's truck

Down
1. Nicodemus's best friend growing up
2. Rats get this through the maze floor when they go the wrong way.
3. Young female rat Mrs. Frisby encounters in the library
4. Mrs. Frisby's husband; also one of the mice
5. Where Mrs. Frisby waits for her first meeting with Nicodemus.
6. Most important skill the rats learn in NIMH
8. Justin read instructions telling how to open the ___ door.
9. Estate where the rats stayed after NIMH
14. The rats spent their time reading and learning to ___ at Boniface Estate.
15. Location of Mrs. Frisby's hiding hole: fence ___
17. Isabella thinks Mrs. Frisby is one.
18. Farming tool Nicodemus designs for the rats to use

MATCHING 1 Mrs. Frisby and the Rats of NIMH

___ 1. TWENTY   A. The Plan is to learn to live without ___.
___ 2. STEALING   B. Place Nicodemus wants to move the rat colony: ___ Valley
___ 3. JENNER   C. Thorny covering over the entrance to the rat hole: rose ___
___ 4. SHOCK   D. Set of corridors Nicodemus ran through while George watched
___ 5. SCHULTZ   E. Doctor who runs NIMH
___ 6. THREAD   F. Number of rats that escaped from NIMH
___ 7. BROOK   G. Justin read instructions telling how to open the ___ door.
___ 8. BUSH   H. Rats get this through the maze floor when they go the wrong way.
___ 9. FITZGIBBON   I. The rats used this when exploring the air ducts.
___ 10. GEORGE   J. Male assistant in the NIMH lab
___ 11. HOUSE   K. Nicodemus's best friend growing up
___ 12. JUSTIN   L. Mrs. Frisby worries about this while Timothy is sick: ___ Day
___ 13. LIBRARY   M. The farmer
___ 14. SPY   N. Estate where the rats stayed after NIMH
___ 15. READING   O. The Frisbys must move from theirs in the garden.
___ 16. THORN   P. Isabella thinks Mrs. Frisby is one.
___ 17. MAZE   Q. He helps Mrs. Frisby escape from Billy.
___ 18. TOY   R. Oldest animal in the woods; he gives advice
___ 19. BILLY   S. Where Mrs. Frisby waits for her first meeting with Nicodemus.
___ 20. OWL   T. Mrs. Frisby's neighbor
___ 21. CAGE   U. He captures Mrs. Frisby under a colander.
___ 22. MOVING   V. The Frisbys' house needs to be moved to the ___ of the stone.
___ 23. BONIFACE   W. Most important skill the rats learn in NIMH
___ 24. LEE   X. The Frisbys live near one in the summer.
___ 25. SHREW   Y. Nicodemus & the rats found tools in his truck: ___ Tinker

ANSWER KEY: MATCHING 1 Mrs. Frisby and the Rats of NIMH

F - 1. TWENTY	A. The Plan is to learn to live without ___.
A - 2. STEALING	B. Place Nicodemus wants to move the rat colony: ___ Valley
K - 3. JENNER	C. Thorny covering over the entrance to the rat hole: rose ___
H - 4. SHOCK	D. Set of corridors Nicodemus ran through while George watched
E - 5. SCHULTZ	E. Doctor who runs NIMH
I - 6. THREAD	F. Number of rats that escaped from NIMH
X - 7. BROOK	G. Justin read instructions telling how to open the ___ door.
C - 8. BUSH	H. Rats get this through the maze floor when they go the wrong way.
M - 9. FITZGIBBON	I. The rats used this when exploring the air ducts.
J - 10. GEORGE	J. Male assistant in the NIMH lab
O - 11. HOUSE	K. Nicodemus's best friend growing up
Q - 12. JUSTIN	L. Mrs. Frisby worries about this while Timothy is sick: ___ Day
S - 13. LIBRARY	M. The farmer
P - 14. SPY	N. Estate where the rats stayed after NIMH
W - 15. READING	O. The Frisbys must move from theirs in the garden.
B - 16. THORN	P. Isabella thinks Mrs. Frisby is one.
D - 17. MAZE	Q. He helps Mrs. Frisby escape from Billy.
Y - 18. TOY	R. Oldest animal in the woods; he gives advice
U - 19. BILLY	S. Where Mrs. Frisby waits for her first meeting with Nicodemus.
R - 20. OWL	T. Mrs. Frisby's neighbor
G - 21. CAGE	U. He captures Mrs. Frisby under a colander.
L - 22. MOVING	V. The Frisbys' house needs to be moved to the ___ of the stone.
N - 23. BONIFACE	W. Most important skill the rats learn in NIMH
V - 24. LEE	X. The Frisbys live near one in the summer.
T - 25. SHREW	Y. Nicodemus & the rats found tools in his truck: ___ Tinker

MATCHING 2 Mrs. Frisby and the Rats of NIMH

___ 1. THREAD
___ 2. OWL
___ 3. READING
___ 4. CHIPMUNKS
___ 5. AGES
___ 6. BROOK
___ 7. LEE
___ 8. POST
___ 9. STUMP
___ 10. SCHULTZ
___ 11. FITZGIBBON
___ 12. STEALING
___ 13. TOOLS
___ 14. THORN
___ 15. PNEUMONIA
___ 16. CARELESS
___ 17. PIN
___ 18. CAGE
___ 19. AIR
___ 20. ISABELLA
___ 21. SHREW
___ 22. MARTIN
___ 23. NEUROLOGIST
___ 24. CIVILIZATION
___ 25. SPY

A. Part Farmer Fitzgibbon orders, which delays plowing: linch ___
B. Oldest animal in the woods; he gives advice
C. The real treasure the rats find in the Toy Tinker's truck
D. Nicodemus wants the rats to build their own ___, just like the Romans & others.
E. Dr. Schultz is one; expert on brains, nerves, intelligence
F. Isabella thinks Mrs. Frisby is one.
G. Location of Mrs. Frisby's hiding hole: fence ___
H. Doctor who runs NIMH
I. Mrs. Frisby's neighbor
J. Six of the mice were blown away by this in the duct.
K. The rats used this when exploring the air ducts.
L. The men said they could capture the rats because they had become ___.
M. The Plan is to learn to live without ___.
N. Most important skill the rats learn in NIMH
O. The farmer
P. Justin read instructions telling how to open the ___ door.
Q. Mrs. Frisby finds corn, nuts, and mushrooms there.
R. They tell Nicodemus to go to the owl.
S. Timothy's older brother
T. Young female rat Mrs. Frisby encounters in the library
U. He makes powders and potions.
V. Timothy's illness
W. The Frisbys live near one in the summer.
X. Place Nicodemus wants to move the rat colony: ___ Valley
Y. The Frisbys' house needs to be moved to the ___ of the stone.

ANSWER KEY: MATCHING 2 Mrs. Frisby and the Rats of NIMH

K - 1. THREAD	A.	Part Farmer Fitzgibbon orders, which delays plowing: linch ___
B - 2. OWL	B.	Oldest animal in the woods; he gives advice
N - 3. READING	C.	The real treasure the rats find in the Toy Tinker's truck
R - 4. CHIPMUNKS	D.	Nicodemus wants the rats to build their own ___, just like the Romans & others.
U - 5. AGES	E.	Dr. Schultz is one; expert on brains, nerves, intelligence
W 6. BROOK	F.	Isabella thinks Mrs. Frisby is one.
Y - 7. LEE	G.	Location of Mrs. Frisby's hiding hole: fence ___
G - 8. POST	H.	Doctor who runs NIMH
Q - 9. STUMP	I.	Mrs. Frisby's neighbor
H -10. SCHULTZ	J.	Six of the mice were blown away by this in the duct.
O -11. FITZGIBBON	K.	The rats used this when exploring the air ducts.
M ·12. STEALING	L.	The men said they could capture the rats because they had become ___.
C -13. TOOLS	M.	The Plan is to learn to live without ___.
X -14. THORN	N.	Most important skill the rats learn in NIMH
V -15. PNEUMONIA	O.	The farmer
L -16. CARELESS	P.	Justin read instructions telling how to open the ___ door.
A -17. PIN	Q.	Mrs. Frisby finds corn, nuts, and mushrooms there.
P -18. CAGE	R.	They tell Nicodemus to go to the owl.
J - 19. AIR	S.	Timothy's older brother
T -20. ISABELLA	T.	Young female rat Mrs. Frisby encounters in the library
I - 21. SHREW	U.	He makes powders and potions.
S -22. MARTIN	V.	Timothy's illness
E -23. NEUROLOGIST	W.	The Frisbys live near one in the summer.
D -24. CIVILIZATION	X.	Place Nicodemus wants to move the rat colony: ___ Valley
F -25. SPY	Y.	The Frisbys' house needs to be moved to the ___ of the stone.

JUGGLE LETTERS 1 Mrs. Frisby and the Rats of NIMH

1. RTEIW = 1. _____
   The rats spent their time reading and learning to ___ at Boniface Estate.

2. IBLYL = 2. _____
   He captures Mrs. Frisby under a colander.

3. WLOP = 3. _____
   Farming tool Nicodemus designs for the rats to use

4. UPHMINSKC = 4. _____
   They tell Nicodemus to go to the owl.

5. GESA = 5. _____
   He makes powders and potions.

6. YTO = 6. _____
   Nicodemus & the rats found tools in his truck: ___ Tinker

7. INRDGEA = 7. _____
   Most important skill the rats learn in NIMH

8. GBIOTZFBIN = 8. _____
   The farmer

9. ROCOLNT = 9. _____
   Group C was the ___ Group.

10. AACYPITC =10. _____
    The size of an animal's brain is no measure of its ___.

11. EELSRACS =11. _____
    The men said they could capture the rats because they had become ___.

12. SBUH =12. _____
    Thorny covering over the entrance to the rat hole: rose ___

13. CTSLHUZ =13. _____
    Doctor who runs NIMH

14. GTHEI =14. _____
    Number of mice the rats freed from their cages

ANSWER KEY: JUGGLE LETTERS 1 Mrs. Frisby and the Rats of NIMH

1. RTEIW = 1. WRITE

   The rats spent their time reading and learning to ___ at Boniface Estate.

2. IBLYL = 2. BILLY

   He captures Mrs. Frisby under a colander.

3. WLOP = 3. PLOW

   Farming tool Nicodemus designs for the rats to use

4. UPHMINSKC = 4. CHIPMUNKS

   They tell Nicodemus to go to the owl.

5. GESA = 5. AGES

   He makes powders and potions.

6. YTO = 6. TOY

   Nicodemus & the rats found tools in his truck: ___ Tinker

7. INRDGEA = 7. READING

   Most important skill the rats learn in NIMH

8. GBIOTZFBIN = 8. FITZGIBBON

   The farmer

9. ROCOLNT = 9. CONTROL

   Group C was the ___ Group.

10. AACYPITC = 10. CAPACITY

    The size of an animal's brain is no measure of its ___.

11. EELSRACS = 11. CARELESS

    The men said they could capture the rats because they had become ___.

12. SBUH = 12. BUSH

    Thorny covering over the entrance to the rat hole: rose ___

13. CTSLHUZ = 13. SCHULTZ

    Doctor who runs NIMH

14. GTHEI = 14. EIGHT

    Number of mice the rats freed from their cages

JUGGLE LETTERS 2 Mrs. Frisby and the Rats of NIMH

1. SLSAEERC = 1. _____
   The men said they could capture the rats because they had become ___.

2. AEZM = 2. _____
   Set of corridors Nicodemus ran through while George watched

3. INP = 3. _____
   Part Farmer Fitzgibbon orders, which delays plowing: linch ___

4. BSFRYI = 4. _____
   She puts the sleeping powder in the cat's bowl.

5. WRESH = 5. _____
   Mrs. Frisby's neighbor

6. USTUBR = 6. _____
   Huge rat revived after breathing the gas.

7. TIERW = 7. _____
   The rats spent their time reading and learning to ___ at Boniface Estate.

8. EIMAOPNUN = 8. _____
   Timothy's illness

9. RDSPIE = 9. _____
   Creature that bit Timothy some time ago

10. ACYIPATC =10. _____
    The size of an animal's brain is no measure of its ___.

11. IARENDG =11. _____
    Most important skill the rats learn in NIMH

12. OPYGR =12. _____
    Yellow canary, once the Fitzgibbons' pet

13. HTEGI =13. _____
    Number of mice the rats freed from their cages

14. TZHSCUL =14. _____
    Doctor who runs NIMH

ANSWER KEY: JUGGLE LETTERS 2 Mrs. Frisby and the Rats of NIMH

1. SLSAEERC = 1. CARELESS
   The men said they could capture the rats because they had become ___.

2. AEZM = 2. MAZE
   Set of corridors Nicodemus ran through while George watched

3. INP = 3. PIN
   Part Farmer Fitzgibbon orders, which delays plowing: linch ___

4. BSFRYI = 4. FRISBY
   She puts the sleeping powder in the cat's bowl.

5. WRESH = 5. SHREW
   Mrs. Frisby's neighbor

6. USTUBR = 6. BRUTUS
   Huge rat revived after breathing the gas.

7. TIERW = 7. WRITE
   The rats spent their time reading and learning to ___ at Boniface Estate.

8. EIMAOPNUN = 8. PNEUMONIA
   Timothy's illness

9. RDSPIE = 9. SPIDER
   Creature that bit Timothy some time ago

10. ACYIPATC =10. CAPACITY
    The size of an animal's brain is no measure of its ___.

11. IARENDG =11. READING
    Most important skill the rats learn in NIMH

12. OPYGR =12. PORGY
    Yellow canary, once the Fitzgibbons' pet

13. HTEGI =13. EIGHT
    Number of mice the rats freed from their cages

14. TZHSCUL =14. SCHULTZ
    Doctor who runs NIMH

VOCABULARY RESOURCE MATERIALS

Mrs. Frisby And The Rats Of NIMH Vocabulary

No.	Word	Clue/Definition
1.	ABREAST	Side by side; beside each other in a line
2.	ABRUPTLY	Suddenly or unexpectedly
3.	ADJOURNED	Suspended (a meeting) until a later time or to another place
4.	ADMONISHED	Mildly scolded; spoken to in disapproval
5.	AGITATED	Troubled or nervous
6.	ARTIFICIAL	Made by human work or art; not by nature
7.	ASTONISHED	Filled with sudden, overpowering surprise or wonder
8.	ASTUTE	Having or showing a clever or shrewd mind
9.	AUTHORITATIVELY	In a commanding way
10.	BEWILDERMENT	The condition of being completely puzzled
11.	CAPTIVITY	Imprisonment
12.	CIRCUMSTANCES	Conditions surrounding an event
13.	CLUTTERED	Containing too many things, and often unorganized
14.	COLANDER	Strainer; a perforated pan used for draining liquids
15.	COMPILED	Made of materials from various sources
16.	COMRADESHIP	Friendship; companionship
17.	CONCEALED	Hidden
18.	CONFER	Have discussions
19.	CONSTERNATION	Great fear or shock that makes one feel helpless
20.	CONTOUR	The outline of a figure, mass, land, etc.
21.	CONVERGED	Came together to meet at a point or in a line
22.	CORDIAL	Courteous; gracious; friendly
23.	CORRIDOR	Passageway giving access to rooms, apartments, etc.
24.	CRYPTICALLY	In a manner that is mysterious or obscure in meaning
25.	CULTIVATED	Prepared for growing crops
26.	CURSORY	Performed rapidly with little attention to detail
27.	CYNICAL	Believing that people are only motivated by selfishness
28.	DEBRIS	Bits and pieces of rubbish; litter
29.	DEFECTIVE	Imperfect; faulty
30.	DELIBERATELY	Intentionally; on purpose; with forethought
31.	DESCENT	The moving from a higher to a lower place
32.	DESPAIRINGLY	In a manner feeling or showing hopelessness
33.	DICTATED	Spoke(n) or read aloud to be written or recorded
34.	DISCONTENT	Dissatisfaction; a restless desire for something more
35.	DISPATCHED	Sent off on a specific errand
36.	DREADFULLY	Terribly
37.	DRONING	Making a continuous, low, monotonous sound
38.	DUSK	Period of partial darkness between day and night as the sun begins to set

No.	Word	Clue/Definition
39.	EAVES	Overhanging, lower edges of a roof
40.	EAVESDROP	Listen secretly to a private conversaion
41.	ELEGANTLY	In a splendid or luxurious style or design
42.	EMERGED	Came forth
43.	EPIDEMIC	Prevalent and spreading rapidly among many individuals
44.	EXERT	Put forth or use energetically
45.	EXPEDITION	Journey or voyage made for a specific purpose
46.	FILTERING	Slipping through slowly as if through an obstruction
47.	FLUTTERED	Waved or flapped about
48.	FRINGES	At the outer edge or border
49.	FUTILE	Incapable of producing any result
50.	GALE	A very strong wind
51.	GRAVELY	Seriously; solemnly
52.	HARROW	Agricultural implement with spike-like teeth or upright disks, for leveling and breaking-up clods in plowed land
53.	HERMIT	Any person living in seclusion
54.	HESITATED	Was reluctant or waited to act because of fear or indecision
55.	HYPODERMIC	Syringe or needle that injects medicine under the skin
56.	ILLOGICAL	Contrary to or disregarding the rules of logic
57.	ILLUSION	Something that deceives by producing a false impression of reality
58.	IMPASSE	A situation offering no escape
59.	INCINERATOR	Furnace or apparatus for burning materials
60.	INCLINE	Slant upward
61.	INCOMPREHENSIBLE	Impossible to understand
62.	INCURRING	Bringing upon oneself
63.	INDIGNANTLY	In a manner expressing great anger or scorn
64.	INEXORABLE	Such that cannot be moved or influenced by persuasion
65.	INEXTRICABLY	In a manner incapable of being disentangled
66.	INKLING	A vague idea or notion
67.	INLAID	Mounted into and flush with the surface of an object
68.	IRRELEVANTLY	In a manner not having anything to do with the matter at hand
69.	IRRIGATION	Means of supplying water via ditches or artificial channels
70.	MANIPULATED	Worked, operated, or treated with the hands
71.	MIDDAY	The middle of the day; noon
72.	PARTITIONS	Dividers
73.	PEDDLER	Person who goes from place to place selling small articles
74.	PERSPIRATION	Sweat
75.	PESSIMIST	Person who sees everything in a negative or the worst possible way

No.	Word	Clue/Definition
76.	PLAINTIVE	Expressing sorrow or melancholy
77.	PLEAD	Make an earnest request
78.	PROSPECT	Outlook for the future
79.	PROTRUDED	Stuck out; extended beyond
80.	RECESSED	Set back
81.	RESPITE	A break
82.	ROUNDABOUT	Circuitous or indirect
83.	ROVING	Wandering about; going from place to place
84.	SATCHEL	Small bag, sometimes with a shoulder strap
85.	SCARCE	Insufficient to satisfy the need or demand
86.	SCURRIED	Scampered or ran hastily
87.	SENTRY	Guard; watch
88.	SHINNY	Climb by using both hands and legs for gripping
89.	SILOS	Airtight pits or towers in which fodder is stored
90.	SKEPTICAL	Doubtful; not easily persuaded or convinced
91.	SPINY	Covered with or having thorns or prickles
92.	STOCKY	Having a sturdy form or build
93.	SUBDUED	Quieted; less active than usual
94.	SUBSIDING	Becoming quieter or less active
95.	SYMPATHETICALLY	In a way showing agreement in feeling
96.	TOILING	Working with exhausting labor or effort
97.	TREMBLING	Shaking involuntarily with quick, short movements as from fear, excitement, or cold
98.	TWINED	Interwoven; wrapped around
99.	UNERRINGLY	Without mistakes
100.	VACANT	Empty
101.	VANTAGE	Position that provides a clear, broad view
102.	VENTILATION	A system that circulates air
103.	VENTURED	Dared to do something dangerous or risky
104.	VIGOROUS	Strong; active; robust
105.	WEARILY	In a tired or worn-out manner
106.	WRITHING	Making twisting or turning movements
107.	YIELDED	Gave way

VOCABULARY WORD SEARCH Mrs Frisby and the Rats of NIMH

```
S A T C H E L E A V E S D R O P T F T B
U I C F Y X K D Y G F R Y T T S S L W G
O A L R N B F A K O B F D I I A U I Q
R R J O Y J I T S N J R C M M N E T N K
O T M P S P N C I M I E I M R E R T E J
G I T N C A T N A N P S N A E X B E D N
I F C R V M G I G L S P C N H O A R N X
V I E D E S S E C E R I L I T R K E V X
A C Q M L M S Y P A Y T I P B A D D Z R
S I B W E V B C I K L E N U V B E Q D M
T A Z R G R B L Y E C L E L D L U Y I I
O L A I A L G Z I O L G Y A V E D S N D
N I G T N A V E N N V D P T B I B C L R
I M I H T I H V D W G M E E N T U R A B
S P T I L D E Q C O R R I D O R S C I Y
H A A N Y R J H V B K K I D R E H A D S
E S T G G O S P A P L G M I V X I P E X
D S E E S C M C C R N Y N A T E N T P F
P E D D L E R F A A R G E M X R N I I S
D L C K L W N X N R S O G S J O Y V D F
K D E I G M Q T T X C T W H P V P I E P
H R T A G F L T R W R E U P J I Y T M L
D U S K D Y C F H Y K C O T S N N Y I R
F P R O S P E C T G A L E W E G J Y C J
```

ABREAST	EAVES	INCURRING	SENTRY
AGITATED	EAVESDROP	INDIGNANTLY	SHINNY
ARTIFICIAL	ELEGANTLY	INEXORABLE	SILOS
ASTONISHED	EMERGED	INLAID	SPINY
ASTUTE	EPIDEMIC	MANIPULATED	STOCKY
CAPTIVITY	EXERT	PEDDLER	SUBDUED
CONVERGED	FLUTTERED	PESSIMIST	TREMBLING
CORDIAL	FRINGES	PLEAD	TWINED
CORRIDOR	FUTILE	PROSPECT	VACANT
CRYPTICALLY	GALE	RECESSED	VANTAGE
CYNICAL	HARROW	RESPITE	VIGOROUS
DEBRIS	HERMIT	ROVING	WRITHING
DRONING	IMPASSE	SATCHEL	YIELDED
DUSK	INCLINE	SCARCE	

ANSWER KEY: VOCABULARY WORD SEARCH Mrs Frisby and the Rats of NIMH

ABREAST	EAVES	INCURRING	SENTRY
AGITATED	EAVESDROP	INDIGNANTLY	SHINNY
ARTIFICIAL	ELEGANTLY	INEXORABLE	SILOS
ASTONISHED	EMERGED	INLAID	SPINY
ASTUTE	EPIDEMIC	MANIPULATED	STOCKY
CAPTIVITY	EXERT	PEDDLER	SUBDUED
CONVERGED	FLUTTERED	PESSIMIST	TREMBLING
CORDIAL	FRINGES	PLEAD	TWINED
CORRIDOR	FUTILE	PROSPECT	VACANT
CRYPTICALLY	GALE	RECESSED	VANTAGE
CYNICAL	HARROW	RESPITE	VIGOROUS
DEBRIS	HERMIT	ROVING	WRITHING
DRONING	IMPASSE	SATCHEL	YIELDED
DUSK	INCLINE	SCARCE	

VOCABULARY CROSSWORD Mrs. Frisby and the Rats of NIMH

Across
1. Overhanging edges of a roof
4. Wandering about; going from place to place
7. Upward slant
10. Person who goes from place to place selling small articles
11. Put forth or use energetically
12. Period of partial darkness between day and night as the sun begins to set
13. Discuss
17. Troubled or nervous
18. Gave way
19. Mounted into and flush with the surface of an object
20. Having a sturdy form or build

Down
1. Listen secretly to a private conversation
2. Empty
3. Climb by using both hands and legs for gripping
4. Set back
5. A very strong wind
6. Outlook for the future
8. Vague idea or notion
9. In a splendid or luxurious style or design
10. Make an earnest request
14. Incapable of producing any result
15. A break
16. Quieted; less active than usual
17. Having or showing a clever or shrewd mind

ANSWER KEY: VOCABULARY CROSSWORD Mrs. Frisby and the Rats of NIMH

Across
1. Overhanging edges of a roof
4. Wandering about; going from place to place
7. Upward slant
10. Person who goes from place to place selling small articles
11. Put forth or use energetically
12. Period of partial darkness between day and night as the sun begins to set
13. Discuss
17. Troubled or nervous
18. Gave way
19. Mounted into and flush with the surface of an object
20. Having a sturdy form or build

Down
1. Listen secretly to a private conversation
2. Empty
3. Climb by using both hands and legs for gripping
4. Set back
5. A very strong wind
6. Outlook for the future
8. Vague idea or notion
9. In a splendid or luxurious style or design
10. Make an earnest request
14. Incapable of producing any result
15. A break
16. Quieted; less active than usual
17. Having or showing a clever or shrewd mind

VOCABULARY MATCHING 1 Mrs Frisby and the Rats of NIMH

___ 1. HYPODERMIC
___ 2. SUBDUED
___ 3. CORRIDOR
___ 4. SPINY
___ 5. INDIGNANTLY
___ 6. RECESSED
___ 7. ELEGANTLY
___ 8. DRONING
___ 9. CYNICAL
___ 10. DREADFULLY
___ 11. HERMIT
___ 12. AGITATED
___ 13. HARROW
___ 14. PARTITIONS
___ 15. GRAVELY
___ 16. INEXTRICABLY
___ 17. DEFECTIVE
___ 18. PLAINTIVE
___ 19. HESITATED
___ 20. ASTUTE
___ 21. TREMBLING
___ 22. AUTHORITATIVELY
___ 23. INEXORABLE
___ 24. PESSIMIST
___ 25. FILTERING

A. In a manner incapable of being disentangled
B. Agricultural implement with teeth or upright disks, for leveling and breaking up dirt clods
C. Slipping through slowly as if through an obstruction
D. Such that cannot be moved or influenced by persuasion
E. Set back
F. Any person living in seclusion
G. Was reluctant or waited to act because of fear or indecision
H. Believing that people are only motivated by selfishness
I. Dividers
J. Shaking involuntarily with quick, short movements as from fear, excitement, or cold
K. Passageway giving access to rooms, apartments, etc.
L. Seriously; solemnly
M. In a manner expressing great anger or scorn
N. Quieted; less active than usual
O. In a commanding way
P. Syringe or needle that injects medicine under the skin
Q. Imperfect; faulty
R. In a splendid or luxurious style or design
S. Person who sees everything in a negative or the worst possible way
T. Having or showing a clever or shrewd mind
U. Terribly
V. Covered with thorns or prickles
W. Expressing sorrow or melancholy
X. Making a continuous, low, monotonous sound
Y. Troubled or nervous

ANSWER KEY: VOCABULARY MATCHING 1 Mrs Frisby and the Rats of NIMH

P - 1.	HYPODERMIC	A.	In a manner incapable of being disentangled
N - 2.	SUBDUED	B.	Agricultural implement with teeth or upright disks, for leveling and breaking up dirt clods
K - 3.	CORRIDOR	C.	Slipping through slowly as if through an obstruction
V - 4.	SPINY	D.	Such that cannot be moved or influenced by persuasion
M - 5.	INDIGNANTLY	E.	Set back
E - 6.	RECESSED	F.	Any person living in seclusion
R - 7.	ELEGANTLY	G.	Was reluctant or waited to act because of fear or indecision
X - 8.	DRONING	H.	Believing that people are only motivated by selfishness
H - 9.	CYNICAL	I.	Dividers
U - 10.	DREADFULLY	J.	Shaking involuntarily with quick, short movements as from fear, excitement, or cold
F - 11.	HERMIT	K.	Passageway giving access to rooms, apartments, etc.
Y - 12.	AGITATED	L.	Seriously; solemnly
B - 13.	HARROW	M.	In a manner expressing great anger or scorn
I - 14.	PARTITIONS	N.	Quieted; less active than usual
L - 15.	GRAVELY	O.	In a commanding way
A - 16.	INEXTRICABLY	P.	Syringe or needle that injects medicine under the skin
Q - 17.	DEFECTIVE	Q.	Imperfect; faulty
W - 18.	PLAINTIVE	R.	In a splendid or luxurious style or design
G - 19.	HESITATED	S.	Person who sees everything in a negative or the worst possible way
T - 20.	ASTUTE	T.	Having or showing a clever or shrewd mind
J - 21.	TREMBLING	U.	Terribly
O - 22.	AUTHORITATIVELY	V.	Covered with thorns or prickles
D - 23.	INEXORABLE	W.	Expressing sorrow or melancholy
S - 24.	PESSIMIST	X.	Making a continuous, low, monotonous sound
C - 25.	FILTERING	Y.	Troubled or nervous

VOCABULARY MATCHING 2 Mrs Frisby and the Rats of NIMH

___ 1. WEARILY   A. Guard; watch
___ 2. ROVING   B. In a tired or worn-out manner
___ 3. YIELDED   C. Troubled or nervous
___ 4. EAVESDROP   D. Put forth or use energetically
___ 5. AUTHORITATIVELY   E. Making twisting or turning movements
___ 6. AGITATED   F. Without mistakes
___ 7. EXERT   G. Listen secretly to a private conversation
___ 8. UNERRINGLY   H. System that circulates air
___ 9. ABRUPTLY   I. Strainer; a perforated pan used for draining liquids
___ 10. SCARCE   J. Having or showing a clever or shrewd mind
___ 11. PEDDLER   K. Terribly
___ 12. INKLING   L. Bits and pieces of rubbish; litter
___ 13. INCINERATOR   M. Gave way
___ 14. ASTUTE   N. The outline of a figure, mass, land, etc.
___ 15. WRITHING   O. Furnace or apparatus for burning materials
___ 16. DREADFULLY   P. Person who goes from place to place selling small articles
___ 17. VENTILATION   Q. Insufficient to satisfy the need or demand
___ 18. COLANDER   R. Made by human work or art, not by nature
___ 19. ABREAST   S. In a commanding way
___ 20. CONTOUR   T. Suddenly or unexpectedly
___ 21. ARTIFICIAL   U. Side by side; beside each other in a line
___ 22. SENTRY   V. Wandering about; going from place to place
___ 23. DEBRIS   W. Vague idea or notion
___ 24. PLEAD   X. Make an earnest request
___ 25. SKEPTICAL   Y. Doubtful; not easily persuaded or convinced

ANSWER KEY: VOCABULARY MATCHING 1 Mrs Frisby and the Rats of NIMH

B - 1. WEARILY	A.	Guard; watch
V - 2. ROVING	B.	In a tired or worn-out manner
M - 3. YIELDED	C.	Troubled or nervous
G - 4. EAVESDROP	D.	Put forth or use energetically
S - 5. AUTHORITATIVELY	E.	Making twisting or turning movements
C - 6. AGITATED	F.	Without mistakes
D - 7. EXERT	G.	Listen secretly to a private conversation
F - 8. UNERRINGLY	H.	System that circulates air
T - 9. ABRUPTLY	I.	Strainer; a perforated pan used for draining liquids
Q -10. SCARCE	J.	Having or showing a clever or shrewd mind
P -11. PEDDLER	K.	Terribly
W 12. INKLING	L.	Bits and pieces of rubbish; litter
O -13. INCINERATOR	M.	Gave way
J - 14. ASTUTE	N.	The outline of a figure, mass, land, etc.
E -15. WRITHING	O.	Furnace or apparatus for burning materials
K -16. DREADFULLY	P.	Person who goes from place to place selling small articles
H -17. VENTILATION	Q.	Insufficient to satisfy the need or demand
I - 18. COLANDER	R.	Made by human work or art, not by nature
U -19. ABREAST	S.	In a commanding way
N -20. CONTOUR	T.	Suddenly or unexpectedly
R -21. ARTIFICIAL	U.	Side by side; beside each other in a line
A -22. SENTRY	V.	Wandering about; going from place to place
L -23. DEBRIS	W.	Vague idea or notion
X -24. PLEAD	X.	Make an earnest request
Y -25. SKEPTICAL	Y.	Doubtful; not easily persuaded or convinced

VOCABULARY JUGGLE LETTERS 1 Mrs Frisby and the Rats of NIMH

1. RGSFEIN = 1. _____
   At the outer edges or border

2. SDIBRE = 2. _____
   Bits and pieces of rubbish; litter

3. CCERSA = 3. _____
   Insufficient to satisfy the need or demand

4. FOENCR = 4. _____
   Discuss

5. NRVOGI = 5. _____
   Wandering about; going from place to place

6. HMESDIPOACR = 6. _____
   Friendship; companionship

7. ELPAITVNI = 7. _____
   Expressing sorrow or melancholy

8. ALDDLUREYF = 8. _____
   Terribly

9. DREESSCE = 9. _____
   Set back

10. REGLYVA =10. _____
    Seriously; solemnly

11. GEEMDER =11. _____
    Came forth

12. ERTNIIOPSPRA =12. _____
    Sweat

13. SOUOVGIR =13. _____
    Strong; active; robust

14. CNILENI =14. _____
    Upward slant

ANSWER KEY: VOCABULARY JUGGLE LETTERS 1 Mrs Frisby and the Rats of NIMH

1. RGSFEIN = 1. FRINGES
   At the outer edges or border

2. SDIBRE = 2. DEBRIS
   Bits and pieces of rubbish; litter

3. CCERSA = 3. SCARCE
   Insufficient to satisfy the need or demand

4. FOENCR = 4. CONFER
   Discuss

5. NRVOGI = 5. ROVING
   Wandering about; going from place to place

6. HMESDIPOACR = 6. COMRADESHIP
   Friendship; companionship

7. ELPAITVNI = 7. PLAINTIVE
   Expressing sorrow or melancholy

8. ALDDLUREYF = 8. DREADFULLY
   Terribly

9. DREESSCE = 9. RECESSED
   Set back

10. REGLYVA = 10. GRAVELY
    Seriously; solemnly

11. GEEMDER = 11. EMERGED
    Came forth

12. ERTNIIOPSPRA = 12. PERSPIRATION
    Sweat

13. SOUOVGIR = 13. VIGOROUS
    Strong; active; robust

14. CNILENI = 14. INCLINE
    Upward slant

VOCABULARY JUGGLE LETTERS 2 Mrs Frisby and the Rats of NIMH

1. EDTROURDP = 1. _____
Stuck out; extended beyond

2. MIICEEPD = 2. _____
Prevalent and spreading rapidly among many individuals

3. MOHIDCYPER = 3. _____
Syringe or needle that injects medicine under the skin

4. TTEDUFERL = 4. _____
Waved or flapped about

5. IPXEEODNIT = 5. _____
Journey or voyage made for a specific purpose

6. UTACDLEVIT = 6. _____
Prepared for growing crops; tended; nurtured

7. SUIORVOG = 7. _____
Strong; active; robust

8. NNLGIKI = 8. _____
Vague idea or notion

9. XIRENLOEAB = 9. _____
Such that cannot be moved or influenced by persuasion

10. EPTISRE =10. _____
A break

11. EJNUDAROD =11. _____
Suspended (a meeting) until a later time or another place

12. VARLGYE =12. _____
Seriously; solemnly

13. VGNODREEC =13. _____
Came together to meet at a point or in a line

14. SANDMHIOED =14. _____
Mildly scolded; spoken to in disapproval

ANSWER KEY: VOCABULARY JUGGLE LETTERS 2 Mrs Frisby and the Rats of NIMH

1. EDTROURDP = 1. PROTRUDED
   Stuck out; extended beyond

2. MIICEEPD = 2. EPIDEMIC
   Prevalent and spreading rapidly among many individuals

3. MOHIDCYPER = 3. HYPODERMIC
   Syringe or needle that injects medicine under the skin

4. TTEDUFERL = 4. FLUTTERED
   Waved or flapped about

5. IPXEEODNIT = 5. EXPEDITION
   Journey or voyage made for a specific purpose

6. UTACDLEVIT = 6. CULTIVATED
   Prepared for growing crops; tended; nurtured

7. SUIORVOG = 7. VIGOROUS
   Strong; active; robust

8. NNLGIKI = 8. INKLING
   Vague idea or notion

9. XIRENLOEAB = 9. INEXORABLE
   Such that cannot be moved or influenced by persuasion

10. EPTISRE = 10. RESPITE
    A break

11. EJNUDAROD = 11. ADJOURNED
    Suspended (a meeting) until a later time or another place

12. VARLGYE = 12. GRAVELY
    Seriously; solemnly

13. VGNODREEC = 13. CONVERGED
    Came together to meet at a point or in a line

14. SANDMHIOED = 14. ADMONISHED
    Mildly scolded; spoken to in disapproval

www.ingramcontent.com/pod-product-compliance
Lightning Source LLC
Chambersburg PA
CBHW051404070526
44584CB00023B/3288